ANTHOLOGY
— for —
MUSIC IN THE NINETEENTH CENTURY

Western Music in Context: A Norton History

Walter Frisch SERIES EDITOR

Music in the Medieval West, by Margot Fassler

Music in the Renaissance, by Richard Freedman

Music in the Baroque, by Wendy Heller

Music in the Eighteenth Century, by John Rice

Music in the Nineteenth Century, by Walter Frisch

Music in the Twentieth and Twenty-First Centuries, by Joseph Auner

ANTHOLOGY
— for —
MUSIC IN THE NINETEENTH CENTURY

Walter Frisch

Columbia University

W. W. NORTON AND COMPANY
NEW YORK · LONDON

Copyright © 2013 by W. W. Norton & Company, Inc.

Editor: Maribeth Payne
Associate Editor: Justin Hoffman
Developmental Editor: Harry Haskell
Manuscript Editor: Jodi Beder
Project Editor: Jack Borrebach
Electronic Media Editor: Steve Hoge
Editorial Assistant: Ariella Foss
Marketing Manager, Music: Amy Parkin
Production Manager: Ashley Horna
Photo Editor: Stephanie Romeo
Permissions Manager: Megan Jackson
Text Design: Jillian Burr
Composition: CMPreparé
Manufacturing: Quad/Graphics—Fairfield, PA

The text of this book is composed in Filosofia OT with the display set in Filosofia OT.

W. W. Norton & Company, Inc., 500 Fifth Avenue, New York, NY 10110-0017
www.wwnorton.com
W. W. Norton & Company, Ltd., Castle House, 75/76 Wells Street, London W1T3QT

1 2 3 4 5 6 7 8 9 0

CONTENTS

Concordance   vii

Preface   ix

1. **Ludwig van Beethoven**: String Quartet in C# Minor, Op. 131, Movements 1 and 2   1

2. **Franz Schubert**: *Gretchen am Spinnrade*, Op. 2 (D. 118)   11

3. **Vincenzo Bellini**: *Norma*, Act 1, Scene 4, *Casta diva*   20

4. **Giacomo Meyerbeer**: *Les Huguenots*, Act 4, Scene 5, Benediction of the Swords   50

5. **Carl Maria von Weber**: *Der Freischütz*, Act 2, Scene 2, *Leise, leise*   77

6. **Felix Mendelssohn**: *Elijah*, Part 2, chorus, *He, watching over Israel*   89

7. **Hector Berlioz**: *Symphonie fantastique*, Movement 2, *Un bal*   97

8. **Franz Liszt**: *Années de pèlerinage I, Suisse*, No. 4, *Au bord d'une source*   124

9. **Frédéric Chopin**: Nocturne in B♭ Minor, Op. 9, No. 1   132

10. **Robert Schumann**: *Dichterliebe*, Op. 48, *Im wunderschönen Monat Mai* and *Aus meinen Tränen sprießen*   139

11. **Hugo Wolf**: *Mörike-Lieder,* No. 24, *In der Frühe*   143

12. **Modest Musorgsky**: *Boris Godunov,* Act 2, Boris's monologue   147

13. **Antonín Dvořák**: Piano Trio No. 4 (*Dumky*), Op. 90, Movement 6   159

14. **Richard Wagner**: *Tristan und Isolde,* Act 1, Scene 3, Isolde's Narrative   169

15. **Giuseppe Verdi**: *Rigoletto,* Act 3, Scene 3, Quartet   189

16. **Georges Bizet**: *Carmen,* Act 1, No. 5, *Habanera*   213

17. **Johannes Brahms**: Symphony No. 1 in C Minor, Op. 68, Movement 1   228

18. **Pyotr Il'yich Tchaikovsky**: Symphony No. 6 in B Minor (*Pathétique*),
    Op. 74, Movement 4   257

19. **Louis Moreau Gottschalk**: *La gallina, danse cubaine*   278

20. **Amy Marcy Cheney Beach**: Violin Sonata in A Minor, Op. 34, Movement 2   285

21. **Gustav Mahler**: *Lieder eines fahrenden Gesellen,* No. 4, *Die zwei blauen Augen*   294

22. **Giacomo Puccini**: *La bohème,* Act 2, Musetta's Waltz   307

23. **Claude Debussy**: *Fêtes galantes* I, *En sourdine*   332

APPENDIX 1 Reading an Orchestral Score   A1

APPENDIX 2 Instrument Names and Abbreviations   A3

APPENDIX 3 Glossary of Performance Indications   A7

CHAPTER 3 | **Music and the Age of Metternich**

Ludwig van Beethoven: String Quartet in C♯ Minor, Op. 131, Movements 1 and 2   1

Franz Schubert: *Gretchen am Spinnrade*, Op. 2 (D. 118)   11

CHAPTER 4 | **The Opera Industry**

Vincenzo Bellini: *Norma*, Act 1, Scene 4, *Casta diva*   20

Giacomo Meyerbeer: *Les Huguenots*, Act 4, Scene 5, Benediction of the Swords   50

Carl Maria von Weber: *Der Freischütz*, Act 2, Scene 2, *Leise, leise*   77

CHAPTER 5 | **Making Music Matter: Criticism and Performance**

Felix Mendelssohn: *Elijah*, Part 2, chorus, *He, watching over Israel*   89

CHAPTER 6 | **Making Music Speak: Program Music and the Character Piece**

Hector Berlioz: *Symphonie fantastique*, Movement 2, *Un bal*   97

Franz Liszt: *Années de pèlerinage I, Suisse*, No. 4, *Au bord d'une source*   124

Frédéric Chopin: Nocturne in B♭ Minor, Op. 9, No. 1   132

Robert Schumann: *Dichterliebe*, Op. 48, *Im wunderschönen Monat Mai* and *Aus meinen Tränen sprießen*   139

CHAPTER 7 | **Beyond Romanticism**

Hugo Wolf: *Mörike-Lieder*, No. 24, *In der Frühe*   143

Modest Musorgsky: *Boris Godunov*, Act 2, Boris's monologue   147

Antonín Dvořák: Piano Trio No. 4 (*Dumky*), Op. 90, Movement 6   159

CHAPTER 8 | **Richard Wagner and Wagnerism**

Richard Wagner: *Tristan und Isolde*, Act 1, Scene 3, Isolde's Narrative   169

CHAPTER 9 | **Verdi, Operetta, and Popular Appeal**

Giuseppe Verdi: *Rigoletto*, Act 3, Scene 3, Quartet   189

Georges Bizet: *Carmen*, Act 1, No. 5, *Habanera*   213

CHAPTER 10 | **Concert Culture and the "Great" Symphony**

Johannes Brahms: Symphony No. 1 in C Minor, Op. 68, Movement 1   228

Pyotr Il'yich Tchaikovsky: Symphony No. 6 in B Minor (*Pathétique*), Op. 74, Movement 4   257

CHAPTER 11 | **Musical Life and Identity in the United States**

Louis Moreau Gottschalk: *La gallina, danse cubaine*   278

Amy Marcy Cheney Beach: Violin Sonata in A Minor, Op. 34, Movement 2   285

CHAPTER 12 | **The Fin de Siècle and the Emergence of Modernism**

Gustav Mahler: *Lieder eines fahrenden Gesellen*, No. 4, *Die zwei blauen Augen*   294

Giacomo Puccini: *La bohème*, Act 2, Musetta's Waltz   307

Claude Debussy: *Fêtes galantes* I, *En sourdine*   332

PREFACE

This anthology is a companion to my book *Music in the Nineteenth Century*, which is part of the series Western Music in Context: A Norton History. The anthology includes scores and analytical commentary for excerpts from a broad range of compositions and can be used on its own or in conjunction with *Music in the Nineteenth Century*.

In *Music in the Nineteenth Century*, like other books in the series, analytical or stylistic discussion of music is expressly kept to a minimum. Yet, as the saying goes, "God lives in the details." No true appreciation of music can be gained by studying social or intellectual context alone. We must engage with the actual notes—the formal structures, the vocal and instrumental writing, the harmonic techniques, the melodic and thematic patterns, and the rhythmic shapes. The commentaries in this anthology provide a pathway to understanding these dimensions of nineteenth-century music. They are not intended to be exhaustive, but rather to invite instructors and students to explore further the works at hand. The commentaries examine formal design (often with the aid of easy-to-read tables), as well as important aspects of thematic construction, harmony, and texture or timbre. For texted works, including songs and operatic excerpts, particularly close attention is paid to the relationships between word and music.

An anthology of this kind, no matter how large, can never be fully representative of the diversity of a period as rich as the nineteenth century, but the present volume offers a good sampling of composers, works, and genres from this era. The repertory includes opera, oratorio, song, and works for piano, chamber ensemble, and orchestra. Chronologically the selections traverse the nineteenth century from 1814 to 1896, and geographically from the U.S. to Western and Eastern Europe.

Students, instructors, and other music lovers have available to them today a number of score anthologies that include music of the nineteenth century. Selections from some major works of the period, including Berlioz's *Symphonie fantastique* or Schumann's *Dichterliebe*, appear in other anthologies as well as here. Some overlap of this kind is inevitable unless we seek to avoid such pillars of the repertory. But I have also chosen works, and excerpts from standard repertoire, that do not appear elsewhere and that illustrate a particular topic or trend discussed in the text.

A wide range of recording options gives students and instructors flexibility in listening to anthology selections. StudySpace, Norton's online resource for students, provides links to stream nearly every anthology selection from Naxos (accessible via an institutional or individual subscription), as well as links to purchase and download recordings from iTunes and Amazon.

All translations are my own unless otherwise indicated. I have attempted to present song texts and opera libretti in a form as close as possible to that in which the writers prepared them—including line breaks, punctuation, and spacing. But the libretto excerpts also reflect the adjustments and additions that composers always made (often with the collaboration of the librettist).

I wish to thank Simon Frisch, Matthew Gelbart, Kevin Karnes, and Marilyn McCoy, all of whom read through the drafts of the commentaries and offered excellent suggestions and advice. Jack Borrebach and Justin Hoffman at W. W. Norton showed both great patience and expertise in helping assemble or set the scores and in coordinating the production of the anthology.

Walter Frisch

ANTHOLOGY

— *for* —

MUSIC IN THE NINETEENTH CENTURY

String Quartet in C♯ Minor, Op. 131: Movements 1 and 2

String quartet, 1826

From Ludwig van Beethoven, *Complete String Quartets*. New York: Dover Publications, Inc.

One of a group of five string quartets that Beethoven wrote late in life, the C♯-Minor Quartet was completed in 1826, a year before the composer's death. With its richness of innovation in form, harmonic and melodic style, and texture, it is in many ways the summation of Beethoven's achievements in the Viennese Classical style of instrumental music. The quartet is distinctive for embedding the four traditional movement types within a larger structure of seven numbered sections, all played without a break.

The first and second movements fulfill in part the roles of a slow introduction and fast sonata form, but the normal proportions are reversed: a slow fugue of about eight minutes gives way to a dancelike movement in sonata form that is less than half as long. In Beethoven's era the fugue, with its evocation of Baroque contrapuntal practice, represented the "learned" or more academic style. Here Beethoven evokes that idiom but then undercuts it in an ironic way by following it with the lively, skittish dance. The relationship between the keys is also unusual and highly un-Classical: the fugue is in C♯ minor, the next movement a half step higher, in D major, the key of the Neapolitan.

The presentation of the first movement's theme in all four voices (mm. 1–16) resembles the exposition of a subject in a traditional fugue. But thereafter Beethoven avoids the conventional Baroque structural division into expositions and freer episodes. Instead, the subject becomes separated into its two component motives:

Each of these motives, which are sometimes further fragmented in a way characteristic of Beethoven, is treated to transformation and modulation that are typical of a development section in a sonata form. Extended sequences, especially with motive **b**, carry the movement into remote key areas. Beethoven also clearly evokes Baroque fugal devices, including inversion (motive **b** in mm. 84–89, played in counterpoint with the original form), diminution (motive **b** in mm. 55ff. and 91ff.), and augmentation (entire subject in cello, mm. 99–107). The final portion of the fugue, from m. 91, is at once a kind of return, or free recapitulation, and a coda: it settles into the main key area of C♯ minor, and the complete fugue subject is heard in several voices for the first time since the initial exposition.

In a way characteristic of late Beethoven, the opening fugue of Op. 131 hovers in a zone between tonality and modality, here because of the strong presence of D♮ on both a small scale (as a melodic note) and large scale (as a harmonic goal). This D could be considered either a Neapolitan inflection (the lowered second degree) within C♯ minor or part of a C♯-Phrygian scale. The second subject entry (or answer) in the fugue begins not a fourth below the subject, as would be expected, but a fifth below. This brings the *sforzando* accent onto the note D♮ (second violin, m. 6), as if shining an aural spotlight on that pitch. Throughout the movement, D major seems to replace or displace the conventional dominant as a harmonic goal. The fugue moves restlessly through a number of tonal areas, finally settling on A major (m. 63; the key signature changes in m. 60), which serves as V of D major, a key reached in measure 73 and made to seem stable because it has been prepared by its own dominant. After a quietly meditative and sparsely scored passage in this key, Beethoven returns to tonic C♯ minor, beginning with the change of key signature in measure 83.

Near the end of the fugue, the role of D♮ as Neapolitan or Phrygian upper neighbor to C♯ is emphasized one last time (mm. 112–16), and the fugue ends in C♯ major (m. 118–20), perhaps an allusion to the Baroque practice of the "Picardy third." Then as if the magnetic pull of the D can no longer be resisted, a bare C♯, played *pianissimo* by all instruments, is suddenly lifted up a half step, and the Allegro gets underway in D major.

The second movement of Op. 131 is in a compact and idiosyncratic sonata form without a development section:

SONATA FORM	Exposition				Recapitulation			Coda
SUBSECTION	Th. 1	trans.	Th. 2	trans.	Th. 1	trans.	Th. 2	
KEY	D		A		D		D	D
MEASURE	1	24	60	74	84	100	133	157

This apparently conventional outline hardly does justice to the movement, whose transparent structure is belied by the quirky themes flowing in the dancelike $\frac{6}{8}$ meter. Understanding the movement is dependent on hearing it in relation to the preceding fugue. Having pulled the quartet from C♯ into D to begin the Allegro, Beethoven soon reminds us whence we came: in the transition (mm. 44–48) the music seems to get stuck on a C♯-major chord, which is sustained by a fermata and animated by a motivic figure C♯–D–C♯ that brings the Neapolitan relationship back into relief. Then, as if snapping out of a reverie, Beethoven moves purposefully toward the "right" key for the second group, the dominant A major, which is prepared by its own dominant E (mm. 48–49).

With such tonal and thematic procedures Beethoven seeks to integrate the movements of an instrumental work and make them part of a larger organic whole. The elusive Allegro is too brief to stand alone as a movement; its identity is bound up with what came before and what will follow.

Gretchen am Spinnrade, Op. 2 (D. 118)

Lied, 1814

From *Franz Schuberts Werke: Kritisch durchgesehene Gesamtausgabe*. Leipzig: Breitkopf & Härtel.

Grab, die gan — ze Welt ____ ist mir ____ ver —

güllt, mein ar — — mer Kopf ____ ist mir ____ ver —

rückt, ____ mein ar — — mer Sinn ____ ist mir ____ zer —

stückt. Mei — ne Ruh' ____ ist

hin, mein Herz ____ ist schwer, ich fin — de, ich

Meine Ruh' ist hin,	*My peace is gone,*
Mein Herz ist schwer,	*My heart is heavy,*
Ich finde sie nimmer	*I'll never find peace,*
Und nimmermehr.	*Ever again.*
Wo ich ihn nicht hab'	*Where he's not with me,*
Ist mir das Grab,	*It's like a tomb,*
Die ganze Welt	*The world around me*
Ist mir vergällt.	*Is a bitter place.*
Mein armer Kopf	*My poor head*
Ist mir verrückt,	*Is crazy to me,*
Mein armer Sinn	*My poor senses*
Ist mir zerstückt.	*Are torn apart.*
Meine Ruh' ist hin,	*My peace is gone,*
Mein Herz ist schwer,	*My heart is heavy,*
Ich finde sie nimmer	*I'll never find peace,*
Und nimmermehr.	*Ever again.*
Nach ihm nur schau ich	*For him only, I look*
Zum Fenster hinaus,	*Out the window,*
Nach ihm nur geh ich	*For him only, I go*
Aus dem Haus.	*Out of the house.*
Sein hoher Gang,	*His lofty bearing,*
Sein' edle Gestalt,	*His noble air,*
Seines Mundes Lächeln,	*The smile on his lips,*
Seiner Augen Gewalt,	*The strength of his gaze,*
Und seiner Rede	*And his talk's*
Zauberfluß,	*Magic flow,*
Sein Händedruck,	*The touch of his hand,*
Und ach, sein Kuß!	*And, ah, his kiss!*
Meine Ruh' ist hin,	*My peace is gone,*
Mein Herz ist schwer,	*My heart is heavy,*
Ich finde sie nimmer	*I'll never find peace,*
Und nimmermehr.	*Ever again.*
Mein Busen drängt sich	*My heart pines*
Nach ihm hin.	*For him.*

Ach dürft ich fassen	*Ah, if I could touch him*
Und halten ihn,	*And hold him,*

Und küssen ihn,	*And kiss him*
So wie ich wollt,	*All I wanted,*
An seinen Küssen	*In his kisses*
Vergehen sollt'!	*I would be lost!*

Meine Ruh' ist hin,	*My peace is gone,*
Mein Herz ist schwer.	*My heart is heavy.*

—Johann Wolfgang von Goethe, *Faust*, Part I.

Schubert's *Gretchen am Spinnrade*, composed in 1814 when he was only 17 years old, is among his earliest settings of poetry by Goethe. Schubert would turn to Goethe's poetry for over 75 songs, or lieder. This poem comes from the first part of Goethe's large verse drama *Faust*, published in 1808. The character Margarete (Gretchen is the diminutive form of the name) is sitting alone in her room at her spinning wheel, thinking of Faust, the man whom she has just met and with whom she has fallen deeply in love.

In his setting, Schubert captures the complicated mix of feelings—agitation, longing, and sorrow—with a musical power unsurpassed since his day. Characteristically, Schubert reaches inside the song, or into the context of the poem, for a central image. From this he creates a musical figure or texture that is featured throughout the song as a unifying device. Here that image is the spinning wheel, which Schubert depicts musically in realistic detail. The right hand of the piano represents the wheel itself, revolving continuously in a circular figuration. The left hand captures the regular motion of the foot on the treadle or pedal, which keeps the wheel in motion. In the course of the song, as Gretchen's fantasy takes hold, she becomes less conscious of her physical actions at the wheel. When she imagines Faust's physical features—his bearing, his manner—Schubert changes the left hand to sustained octaves and fifths (m. 51). And when she mentions Faust's kiss (mm. 66–68), the wheel seems to stop altogether, frozen into a diminished seventh chord sustained by a fermata. Then, as Gretchen comes back to herself and to reality, the left hand of the pianist reactivates the treadle; and slowly, over three measures, the spinning wheel resumes its regular motion (mm. 69–73).

Harmonically Schubert's song shows both adherence to and departure from Classical norms. The main contrasting key is F major (m. 51), a conventional goal for a piece in D minor. But near the beginning of the song Schubert creates tonal ambiguities more characteristic of the Romantic era. In measure 7 the tonic D minor drops by whole step to C major, which we might expect to serve as V of F, but which just sits there in a static fashion before returning to D minor in measure 13. It returns via a brief A chord (second half of m. 12) that, again according to expectation, should have a C♯ and function as V of D minor, but remains without any third—just the open fifth A–E. These kinds of harmonic techniques, which bypass conventional progressions, become typical of the Romantic period.

The form of *Gretchen am Spinnrade* is unique. It is neither strophic nor through-composed, but a special fusion of the two. There is a musical refrain that always appears in the tonic key (mm. 1, 31, 73, 114). At each occurrence except the last, the music following the refrain leads off in new directions, to different keys and melodic motives. The song thus unfolds like a series of ever-widening arches. This process also includes the voice's melodic range, which gradually expands. Schubert plots the high notes to rise from F (mm. 10, 39, 61), to G (m. 68), and to A (mm. 107, 111) at the climax.

Schubert does not hesitate to alter Goethe's poetry where it will serve him musically to do so. Schubert repeats the last stanza of the poem in mm. 101–12, altering the first line to "O könnt' ich ihn küssen" (Oh, if I could kiss him). He also brings back the first part of the refrain one last time in measure 114, as a kind of coda. This final appearance of the lines "Meine Ruh' ist hin / Mein Herz ist schwer" is not in Goethe's original poem. The additional text is set to music that expresses Gretchen's utter exhaustion: her spinning song is over, but her anguish remains unresolved. In transforming the poetry into song, Schubert needed these repetitions in order to create a musical climax and then a winding down.

3

VINCENZO BELLINI (1801–1835)

Norma: Casta diva, Act 1, Scene 4

Opera, 1831

From Vincenzo Bellini, *Norma*. Milan: Ricordi.

16 NORMA

Ca _ _ _ _ sta Di _ _ _va, ca _ sta Di _ va, che i _ nar _

19 N

_gen _ ti que _ _ _ ste sa _ cre, que _ ste

22 N

sa _ cre, queste sa _ cre an _ tiche pian _ te, a noi vol _ gi il bel sem _

25 N

_bian _ te, a __ noi vol _ gi, a noi vol _ gi il bel sem _ bian _ _ _ _ _ _

sempre cresc. sino al.....

sempre cresc. sino al..........

- - - - -te, il bel sem _ bian _ te sen _ za nu _ bee sen _ za

vel,

OROVESO
Ca _ _ _ sta   Di _ _ _

Soprani
Ca _ sta Di _ va, che i _ nar _ gen _ ti que _ ste sa _ creanti _ che

sottovoce
Tenori
Ca _ sta Di _ va, che i _ nar _ gen _ ti que _ ste sa _ creanti _ che

Bassi
Ca _ _ _ sta   Di _ _ _

dolce espressivo e *ppp* sempre

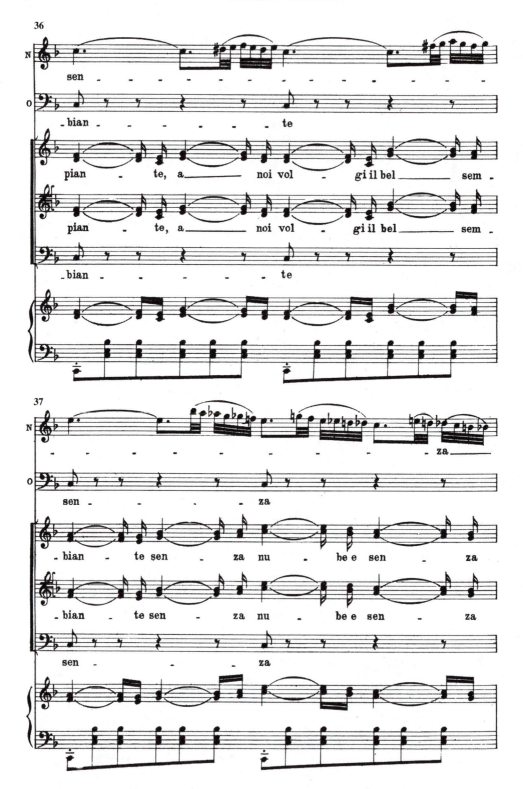

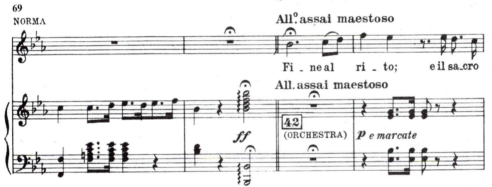

fo _ sco chiegga il san _ gue dei Ro _ ma _ ni, dal dru _

_ i _ di _ co de _ lu _ bro __ la __ mia __ vo _ _ ce

tuo _ _ ne _ rà.

OROVESO

Tuo _ ni; e un sol del po _ pol

Soprani

Tuo _ ni; e un sol __ del __ po _ pol __

Tenori

Tuo _ ni; e un sol __ del __ po _ pol __

Bassi

Tuo _ ni; e un sol del po _ pol

118

bel _ lo a me_____ ri _ tor _ _ na del__

120   con forza

rag _ gio tuo__ se _ re _ no;   e vi _ ta_ nel tuo

Opp.

se _ no_ e pa _

123   con abbandono

se _ no   e   pa _ _ _ _ tria e cie _ lo a _

pp

129 Brackets indicate cuts in recorded performance

gior _ no di ven _ det _ ta; ma i _ ra _ to il Dio t'af _

gior _ no di ven _ det _ ta; ma i _ ra _ to il Dio t'af _

gior _ no di ven _ det _ ta; ma i _ ra _ to il Dio t'af _

gior _ no di ven _ det _ ta; ma i _ ra _ to il Dio t'af _

_fret _ ta che il Te _ bro con _ dan _ nò, ma i _

_fret _ ta che il Te _ bro con _ dan _ no, ma i _

_fret _ ta che il Te _ bro con _ dan _ nò, ma i _

_fret _ ta che il Te _ bro con _ dan _ nò, ma i _

fe - sa a ___ te sa __ rò. Ah! __

bel - lo a me ___ ri tor __ na del __

rag - gio tuo __ se - re - no; e vi - ta nel tuo

PREGHIERA (PRAYER)

[CANTABILE]

NORMA AND MINISTERS

Casta Diva, che inargenti	*Pure Goddess, who silvers*
queste sacre antiche piante,	*these sacred ancient plants,*
a noi volgi il bel sembiante	*turn thy beautiful semblance on us*
senza nube e senza vel.	*unclouded and unveiled.*
Tempra, o Diva, tu de' cori ardenti	*Temper, o Goddess, their burning hearts*
tempra ancora lo zelo audace,	*temper as well their brave zeal,*
spargi in terra quella pace	*scatter on the earth the peace*
che regnar tu fai nel ciel.	*you make reign in the heavens.*

ALL

A noi volgi il bel sembiante
senza nube e senza vel.

Turn thy beautiful semblance on us
unclouded and unveiled.

[TEMPO DI MEZZO]

NORMA

Fine al rito: e il sacro bosco
sia disgombro dai profani.
Quando il Nume irato e fosco,
chiegga il sangue dei Romani,
dal Druidico delubro
la mia voce tuonerà.

The rite is over: let the sacred wood
be clear of the laity.
When the irate and gloomy God
asks for the blood of the Romans
from the Druidic temple
my voice will thunder.

ALL

Tuoni; e un sol del popolo empio
Non isfugga al giusto sempio;
E primier da noi percosso
il proconsole cadrà.

Let it thunder, let not a single impious person
be spared from your just wrath;
and the first to be struck by us,
the proconsul will fall.

NORMA

Sì: cadrà . . . punirlo io posso. . .
(ma, punirlo, il cor non sa.)

Yes, he will fall; I can punish him,
(but my heart is unable to do it.)

[CABALETTA]

(Ah! bello a me ritorna
del fido amor primiero;
e contro il mondo intiero
difesa a te sarò.
Ah! bello a me ritorna
del raggio tuo sereno;
e vita nel tuo seno,
e patria e cielo avrò.)

(Ah! handsome one, return to me,
to your first true love;
and against the entire world
I will be your defense.
Ah! handsome one, return to me
with your serene appearance;
and in your heart I will have life,
fatherland, and sky.)

CHORUS

Sei lento, sì, sei lento,	*You come slowly, yes, you come slowly*
o giorno di vendetta;	*o day of vengeance;*
ma irato il dio t'affretta	*but an angry God hurries you on*
che il Tebro condannò.	*whom the Tiber condemns.*

NORMA

(Ah, riedi ancora	*(Oh! return again*
qual eri allora,	*to what you were then,*
quando il cor ti diedi	*when I gave you my heart,*
allora riedi a me.)	*Now return to me.)*

Norma leaves, and all follow her in order.

—Felice Romani; with additions by Bellini.

Norma was the ninth of eleven operas written by Vincenzo Bellini in a career cut tragically short by his death at the age of 33. With a libretto by Bellini's regular collaborator Felice Romani, *Norma* is a splendid example of early Romantic Italian opera in what has been called the bel canto tradition. The solo singing voice is the center of musical attention, with displays of lyricism and virtuosity.

But emphasis on the voice does not mean the absence of drama, which, in the works of Bellini, Donizetti, and their immediate successor Verdi, is often carried by musical units that are closed on the largest level—and thus are "numbers"—but comprise several continuous sections. *Casta diva* is an example of one such structure, the "scena ed aria" (scene and aria), or "scena e cavatina" (the term "cavatina" designates an aria-like number). *Casta diva* is also, as Romani specifies, a "preghiera" or prayer, a type of number frequently encountered in Romantic opera in which a hero or heroine asks for divine guidance in a moment of trouble. In this prayer, Norma, the Druid priestess, is joined by the chorus of Druids and their leader (and her father) Oroveso.

Casta diva has a characteristic four-part design, though not labeled as such by composer or librettist. Part 1, which is not included in the excerpt here, is sometimes called the "tempo d'attacco" (beginning movement); it combines recitative and more melodic phrases. Part 2 is a slow lyrical portion commonly referred to as the "cantabile" (marked in the libretto above), which is preceded by a long instrumental introduction. Part 3 is a section in freer form more like the first, called "tempo di mezzo" (middle movement). Part 4 is a "cabaletta," a fast concluding segment often featuring vocal pyrotechnics from the soloist. The cabaletta is usually repeated.

As is typical in a *scena ed aria*, the structure of *Casta diva* depends on the introduction of a new plot element or information in Part 3, to which the main character reacts in Part 4. In (1) Norma says it is not yet time for the Gauls to rise up against their Roman occupiers.

In (2) she offers a hymnlike prayer to the chaste moon goddess, and her prayer is taken up by the chorus and Oroveso. In part (3) of *Casta diva*, the mood changes to one of defiance as the Druids demand that the first Roman victim be Pollione, whom they do not know was once Norma's lover and is the father of her two children. In the fast and virtuosic cabaletta, (4), which she sings to herself as an aside, a conflicted Norma confesses that she cannot sacrifice Pollione.

Romani constructed his libretto carefully according to this dramatic-formal scheme. The cantabile and tempo di mezzo use the *ottonario* line, an eight-syllable Italian verse form. For the cabaletta, Romani uses a shorter *settenario*, or seven-syllable line, which is better suited to the fast tempo. To mark the ending of a stanza, the last line is sometimes truncated by one syllable, and is thus called a *tronco*. For musical reasons—to fill out a phrase, or to emphasize certain emotions—Bellini and his contemporaries typically added some words, exclamations, or even whole verses, as can be seen in the bracketed passages.

The cantabile of *Casta diva* is characteristic of Bellini's long lyrical lines, in which what might ordinarily be distinguished as "melody" and "ornament" are tightly integrated. The shorter decorative notes are part of the musical structure. The main theme of the cantabile extends over 15 measures (mm. 16–30), and is divided into shorter units, as is characteristic for Italian opera. First come two parallel four-measure phrases, **A** (mm. 16–19) and **A′** (mm. 20–23), oriented around the tonic F. Then a contrasting **B** phrase (mm. 24–25) moves to a diminished seventh harmony. Bellini returns to the tonic at measure 26, but instead of resuming **A**, as would be expected, the melody deviates (thus **C**) and soars upward to a huge climax, *fortissimo* on a high B♭, before sinking back to the tonic note and harmony F in measure 30, where the chorus enters.

The recording of *Casta diva* available on StudySpace was made in 1954 by the great soprano Maria Callas, with the conductor Tullio Serafin, at Opera of La Scala in Milan. As has always been common in performances of bel canto opera, some alterations were made in the score. Here Callas and Serafin omit the repeat of the cabaletta (mm. 129–60) and a portion of closing segment (mm. 172–79). These passages are bracketed in our score. Like all prima donnas, Callas also embellishes or adjusts some passages to show off her vocal prowess. Most striking (indeed, thrilling) is the high C she sings in m. 186 at the final cadence, in place of Bellini's B♭.

4

GIACOMO MEYERBEER (1791–1864)

Les Huguenots: Act 4, Scene 5, Benediction of the Swords
Opera, 1836

From Giacomo Meyerbeer, *Les Huguenots*. Paris: G. Brandus, Dufour.

_re au guerrier fi_dè _le,_

Dont le glaive é_tin_cel _le Pour servir le Seigneur, Dont le glaive é_tin_

(sans le 1.er Moine)

_cel _le Pour servir le Sei_gneur!

(Tous les assistants tirent leurs épées et leurs poignards; les moines bénissent les armes

S.t BRIS et les 3 Moines (étendant les mains)

81

_tié! Frappez tous _____ sans re_là_che, L'ennemi _____ qui s'en

83

_fuit, l'ennemi _____ qui se cache,

ff

Frappons, frappons, frap_ pons, frappons, frappons, frap_

Frappons, frappons, frap_ pons, frappons, frappons, frap_

Frappons, frappons, frap _ pons, frappons, frappons, frap

flamme Attei _ _ _ guent le vieillard   et l'enfant _ _ _ _ _ _ et la

fem _ me!   Ana _ thè _ me sur eux!   Ana _ thè _ me sur

Ana _ thè _ me sur

Ana _ thè _ me sur

Ana _ thè _ me sur

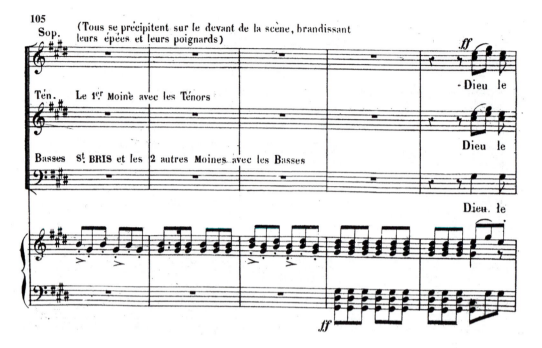

158

162

Dieu,   à mon Dieu, à mon roi! _____ Comp _ tez   sur   mon   cou_

Dieu,   à mon Dieu, à mon roi! _____ Comp _ tez   sur   mon   cou_

Dieu,   à mon Dieu, à mon roi! _____ Comp _ tez   sur   mon   cou_

_ra _ ge; En _ tre vos mains j'en _ ga _ ge,   en_

_ra _ ge; En _ tre vos mains j'en _ ga _ ge,   en_

_ra _ ge; En _ tre vos mains j'en _ ga _ ge,   en_

_tre vos mains j'en-ga-ge Mes ser_ments, mes serments et ma

_tre vos mains j'en-ga-ge Mes ser_ments, mes serments et ma

_tre vos mains j'en-ga-ge Mes ser_ments, mes serments et ma

foi!   A minuit! (Tous se retirent lentement)   Point de bruit!

foi!

foi!   A minuit!

The doors at the back open; three monks carrying baskets with white scarves advance slowly. Saint-Bris accompanies them.

THREE MONKS

Gloire au Dieu Vengeur!	*Glory to God the Avenger!*
Gloire au guerrier fidèle	*Glory to the faithful soldier*
Dont le glaive étincelle	*Whose blade flashes*
Pour servir le Seigneur!	*To serve the Lord!*

All who are present draw their daggers or swords—the monks bless the weapons.

Glaives pieux, saintes épées,	*Pious blades, sacred swords,*
Qui dans un sang impur serez bientôt trempées,	*Which will soon be soaked in tainted blood,*
Vous par qui les Très-Haut frappe ses ennemis,	*You through which the All-Highest strikes his enemies,*
Glaives pieux, par nous soyez bénis!	*Pious blades, be blessed by us!*

CHORUS

Oui, gloire au Dieu vengeur!	*Yes, glory to God the Avenger!*
Gloire au guerrier fidèle	*Glory to the faithful soldier*
Dont le glaive étincelle	*Whose blade flashes*
Pour servir le Seigneur!	*To serve the Lord!*

SAINT-BRIS
(showing them the white cross and scarf he is wearing)

Que cette écharpe blanche et cette croix sans tache	*May this white scarf and this unblemished cross*
Du ciel distinguent les élus!	*Distinguish the elect of heaven!*

THREE MONKS AND SAINT-BRIS
(each addressing a group)

Ni grâce, ni pitié! Frappez tous sans relâche	*Neither mercy, nor pity! Strike all without pause*
L'ennemi qui s'enfuit, l'ennemi qui se cache,	*The enemy who flees, the enemy who hides,*

CHORUS

Frappons, frappons, frappons!	*Let us strike, let us strike, let us strike!*

THREE MONKS AND SAINT-BRIS

Le guerrier suppliant à vos pieds abbatu!	*The stricken warrior begging at your feet!*

CHORUS

Frappons, frappons, frappons!	*Let us strike, let us strike, let us strike!*

THREE MONKS AND SAINT-BRIS

Ni grâce, ni pitié! que le fer et la flamme	*Neither mercy, nor pity! Let sword and fire*
Atteignent le viellard et l'enfant et la flamme!	*Pierce the old man, the child and the woman!*
Anathème sur eux! Dieu ne les connaît pas!	*A curse upon them! God does not recognize them!*

CHORUS

Dieu le veut! Dieu l'ordonne!	*God wills it! God commands it!*
Non! Non! grâce à personne!	*No one will be spared!*
A ce prix il pardonne	*At this price he pardons*
Au pécheur repentant.	*The sinner who repents.*
Que le glaive étincelle,	*Let the sword flash,*
Que le sang ruisselle,	*Let the blood flow,*
Et la palme immortelle	*And the immortal palm*
Dans le ciel vous attend!	*Awaits you in heaven!*

SAINT-BRIS AND FIRST MONK

Silence, mes amis!	*Silence, my friends!*
Que rien ne nous trahisse,	*Let nothing betray us,*
Retirons-nous sans bruit!	*Let us withdraw without noise!*

The monks signal those present to kneel, and then bless them, moving among the different groups.

THE CHORUS

Pour cette cause sainte	*For this sacred cause*
J'obéirai sans crainte	*Fearlessly I will obey*
A mon Dieu, à mon roi!	*My God and my king!*
Comptez sur mon courage,	*Count on my courage,*
Entre vos mains j'engage	*In your hands I place*
Mes serments et ma foi!	*My vow and my faith!*
A minuit! Point de bruit!	*Until midnight! No noise!*
Que rien ne nous trahisse,	*Let nothing betray us,*
Et que de leur supplice	*And of their torment*
Rien ne les avertisse!	*Let nothing alert them!*
Retirons-nous!	*Let us withdraw!*
Point de bruit! A minuit!	*No noise! Until midnight!*
Dieu le veut! Oui!	*God wills it. Yes!*
A minuit!	*Until midnight!*

The crowd files out in silence. Saint-Bris departs with them.

—Eugène Scribe

Giacomo Meyerbeer was an international figure in European music in the first half of the nineteenth century, a German who took on an Italian first name when he went to work in Italy, then later made his career primarily in France. Working with the impresario of the Paris Opéra, Louis Véron, and the librettist Eugene Scribe, Meyerbeer developed the genre known as French grand opera, which relied on historical plots with religious or political themes. Grand opera was a true spectacle, featuring crowd scenes, vivid choruses, lavish costumes, and elaborate sets and lighting.

Les Huguenots (1836) is based on the story of the massacre of Huguenots (French Protestants) by Catholics in Paris on the night preceding the feast of St. Bartholomew, August 24, 1572. The violent conflict between Catholics and Protestants lies at the heart of the opera, as does the secret relationship between two lovers of the opposing faiths, Raoul and Valentine.

One of the best-known scenes in *Les Huguenots* comes in Act 4, where the Count de Saint-Bris and his fellow Catholic noblemen plan the demise of the Protestants. The scene is dominated by bold rhythmic ideas, stirring melodies, and declamatory outbursts from the chorus—all on the large scale that Meyerbeer exploited to great effect. Monks arrive with white scarves to be worn by the Catholics. An oath is taken as the swords are ceremonially blessed, to the accompaniment of solemn chords. The conspirators express defiance and invoke "God the Avenger" in their violent cause. The scene ends with a hymnlike tune sung in unison by the entire ensemble before they steal away in conspiratorial silence.

Characteristically for grand opera, there is emphasis on the visual element—here the blessing of the swords. No composer was better than Meyerbeer at rendering such symbolic moments in music. Meyerbeer exploits the world of Romantic harmony to dramatic effect, especially relations by thirds, which take precedence over traditional tonic–dominant progressions. The scene begins in the key of A♭ and ends in E major, a major third lower (the flatted sixth degree). During the blessing of the swords and Saint-Bris's response (mm. 27–42), Meyerbeer starkly juxtaposes these two chords, as well as the chord of C major, which lies a major third on the other side of A♭.

The second part of the scene ("Dieu le veut," m. 104) turns to a faster tempo and a more fluid ⁶₈ meter, and the key signature changes to E major. But resolution to that key is a long time coming: the segment begins in G♯ minor, which is the enharmonic equivalent of A♭ minor and thus the darker side of the key of the first part. Meyerbeer frequently inflects the music back to A♭ major (as in the softer choral passage "Et la palme immortelle," mm. 126–30). When the chorus kneels to receive the final blessing of the monks (m. 177), the music turns at last to E major and to a more spacious quadruple meter for the noble, hymnlike "Pour cette cause sainte," which is the reprise of a theme heard in the previous scene.

CARL MARIA VON WEBER (1786–1826)

Der Freischütz: Act 2, Scene 2, Leise, leise

Opera, 1821

From Carl Maria von Weber, *Der Freischütz*. New York: Kalmus.

Wei - se, schwing' dich auf zum Ster-nen-krei - se! Lied, er - schal - le,

Vc. *pp*

fei - ernd wal - le mein Ge-bet zur Him-mels-hal - le!

Recit. (looking out)

O wie hell die gold'-nen Ster - ne, mit wie rei - nem Glanz sie glüh'n! Nur dort in der Ber - ge Fer - ne scheint ein

Va., D.B.

Wet - ter auf - zu - zieh'n, dort am Wald auch schwebt ein Heer dun - kler Wol - ken dumpf und

Adagio.

schwer. Zu dir wen - de ich die Hän - de,

Fl.

Vns. divisi

Cl.

pp

Viola

Herr ohn' An-fang und ohn' En - - de. Vor Ge - fah - ren uns____ zu

wah - ren, sen - de dei-ne_ En - gel - schaa - - ren!

Andante

Al - - les pflegt schon längst der_ Ruh'! Trau - ter Freund, wo wei - lest_

du? Ob mein Ohr auch eif - - rig

lauscht,____ nur der Tan - - nen Wip - - fel

weh'n! Dein Mäd - - chen wacht noch in der

(She waves a white handkerchief to him.)

Recit.

Nacht! Er scheint mich noch nicht zu seh'n,

Gott! täuscht das Licht des Mond's mich nicht, so schmückt ein Blu - men strauss den Hut! Ge -

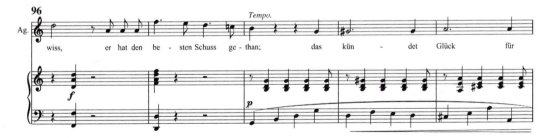

Tempo.

wiss, er hat den be - sten Schuss ge - than; das kün - det Glück für

mor - gen an! O sü - sse Hoff - nung! neu - be - leb - ter

Ob. & Bsn.

158

Ag. ren für dies Pfand der Hoff - nung an!___ Him - mel,___ nimm des___

Cl. sustain

f Tutti

164

Ag. Dan - kes Zäh - ren für___ dies___ Pfand___ der Hoff - nung an!

Fl. & Vln.

ff

170

Ag. All'_ mei - ne Pul - se schla - gen, und das Herz wallt un - ge - stüm,

Winds

ff

174

Ag. all'_ mei - ne Pul - se___ schla - gen,_ und das___ Herz wallt un - ge - stüm___ süss___ ent -

a piacere, ma con

Vln.

Tutti   colla voce

179   *tutta forza*   *a tempo*

Ag. zückt ent - ge - gen ihm,___ ent - ge - gen ihm! süss ent -

Strings

p

poco   a

Bsn.

[RECITATIVE]

AGATHE

Wie nahte mir der Schlummer,	*How did I ever sleep*
Bevor ich ihn geseh'n?	*Before I saw him?*
Ja, Liebe pflegt mit Kummer	*Yes, love gives us anguish*
Stets Hand in Hand zu gehn!	*The two always go hand in hand!*
Ob Mond auf seinem Pfad wohl lacht?	*Is the moon laughing on its path?*

She opens the door to the balcony, revealing a view onto a starlit landscape.

Welch schöne Nacht!	*What a beautiful night!*

She steps onto the balcony and raises her hands with devout emotion.

[ARIA, STROPHE 1]

Leise, leise,	*Softly, softly,*
Fromme Weise!	*My pious melody!*

Schwing' dich auf zum Sternenkreise!	*Soar upward to the starry skies!*
Lied, erschalle!	*Resound, my song!*
Feiernd walle	*Float solemnly,*
Mein Gebet zur Himmelshalle!—	*My prayer to the halls of heaven!—*

[RECITATIVE]

O wie hell die gold'nen Sterne,	*Oh, how clear are the golden stars,*
Mit wie reinem Glanz sie glüh'n!	*They glow with such a pure radiance!*
Nur dort in der Berge Ferne	*Yet over there in the distant mountains*
Scheint ein Wetter aufzuzieh'n.	*A storm seems to be rising.*
Dort am Wald auch schwebt ein Heer	*And there in the forest is moving a cluster*
Dunkler Wolken dumpf und schwer.	*Of dark clouds, stifling and heavy.*

[ARIA, STROPHE 2]

Zu dir wende	*To you I turn*
Ich die Hände,	*My hands,*
Herr ohn' Anfang und ohn' Ende!	*Lord without beginning and end!*
Vor Gefahren	*From danger*
Uns zu wahren	*To preserve us*
Sende deine Engelscharen!—	*Send your hosts of angels!—*

She looks out again.

[ANDANTE]

Alles pflegt schon längst der Ruh':	*Everything has long since gone to rest:*
Trauter Freund! wo weilest du?	*Dear friend! why are you delaying?*
Ob mein Ohr auch eifrig lauscht,	*Even when my ear eagerly listens,*
Nur der Tannen Wipfel rauscht,	*Only the tops of the fir trees rustle,*
Nur das Birkenlaub im Hain	*Only the birch leaves in the grove*
Flüstert durch die hehre Stille;	*Whisper through the glorious silence;*

[RECITATIVE]

Nur die Nachtigall und Grille	*Only the nightingale and cricket*
Scheint der Nachtluft sich zu freu'n.	*Appear to take pleasure in the night air.*
Doch wie? Täuscht mich nicht mein Ohr?	*And yet? Is my ear not deceiving me?*
Dort klingt's wie Schritte—	*It sounds like footsteps!—*

Dort aus der Tannen Mitte	*There, from the middle of the fir trees*
Kommt was hervor—	*Something is coming—*
Er ist's! Er ist's!	*It's him! It's him!*
Die Flagge der Liebe mag weh'n!	*Let the banner of love wave!*

She waves a white handkerchief.

Dein Mädchen wacht	*Your maiden is watching*
Noch in der Nacht—	*Even through the night—*
Er scheint mich noch nicht zu seh'n—	*He doesn't seem to have seen me yet—*
Gott! täuscht das Licht	*God! if the light of the moon*
Des Mond's mich nicht,	*Is not deceiving me,*
So schmückt ein Blumenstrauß den Hut—	*A bouquet of flowers adorns his hat—*
Gewiß, er hat den besten Schuß getan!	*Surely he has made the best shot!*
Das kündet Glück für morgen an!	*That foretells luck for tomorrow!*
O süße Hoffnung! neu belebter Mut!—	*Oh, sweet hope! courage newly revived!—*

[VIVACE CON FUOCO]

Alle meine Pulse schlagen,	*All my pulses are beating,*
Und das Herz wallt ungestüm,	*And my heart churns wildly,*
Süß entzückt entgegen ihm!	*Sweetly enchanted by him!*
Konnt'ich das zu hoffen wagen?—	*Could I dare to hope?—*
Ja, es wandte sich das Glück	*Yes, fortune has returned*
Zu dem teuren Freund zurück,	*To my dear beloved,*
Will sich morgen treu bewähren!	*And will remain true tomorrow!*
Ist's nicht Täuschung? Ist's nicht Wahn?—	*Is it not illusion? Is it not madness?—*
Himmel, nimm des Dankes Zähren	*Heavens, take these tears of thanks*
Für dies Pfand der Hoffnung an!	*For this pledge of hope!*

—Friedrich Kind

Weber's *Der Freischütz* (The Free-Shooter) represents a landmark in German opera, a work that instantly touched national and cultural sensibilities. With a libretto by the playwright and poet Friedrich Kind, the opera is set in the Bohemian forest in central Europe (a largely German-speaking region) during the period after the Thirty Years War in the seventeenth century. The main characters in *Freischütz* are hunters, farmers, and peasants. Weber fills the opera with their sonorities, including hunting horns and choruses, and earthy peasant dances. The title refers to hunter Max, whose magic bullets will always hit their target—with the exception of one, which is under the control of the demonic figure Samiel.

The main female character in *Freischütz* is Agathe, daughter of a forester, who is engaged to Max and embodies the German Protestant values of modest piety. Her main aria, *Leise, leise*, begin with what she identifies as a "pious" (*fromm*) melody. The tune is simple, in the manner of folk music so beloved of Germans in the Romantic period, and it is accompanied by diatonic harmonies.

Agathe's number combines structural and stylistic elements of both Italian and German opera. It resembles a "scena" (like *Casta diva* from Bellini's *Norma*, Anthology 3) in that it is long—lasting over eight minutes in most performances—and features a range of vocal styles, including recitative, arioso, and aria. As in the increasingly standard format for Italian opera numbers from Rossini on (like *Casta diva*), the aria-like section has a slow-fast design on the largest level. But in Weber the slow part (Adagio) is cast as a strophic form in the manner of a folklike German lied. (The two strophes are separated by some recitative, as indicated above.) After an intervening Andante and further recitative comes the Vivace section, where Agathe eagerly anticipates Max's arrival. It has some of the infectious rhythmic drive and elemental harmonic energy of Rossini (rapid I–V bass progressions), and the melody is repeated in the manner of a cabaletta (mm. 118 and 162).

Weber shows a truly Romantic sense of orchestral and harmonic coloring. The Adagio, the strophic song, is scored initially for a delicate string ensemble consisting of muted, divided violins and violas (cellos enter only after eight measures). Horns appear for the Andante, and the full orchestra breaks forth for the Vivace. The key of the Andante, C major, lies a major third away from the E major of the Adagio and Vivace sections, and it is approached directly (mm. 61–62), without the modulation that would be characteristic of the Classical style.

Elijah: Part 2, chorus, *He, watching over Israel*
Oratorio, 1846

From Felix Mendelssohn, *Elijah*. New York: G. Schirmer, Inc.

He, watching over Israel, slumbers not, nor sleeps. Shouldst thou, walking in grief,
languish, He will quicken thee.

—Psalm 121:4; Psalm 138:7

Mendelssohn began planning the oratorio *Elijah* as early as 1836, shortly after he finished his
first oratorio, *St. Paul*. But he was to complete *Elijah* only a decade later in 1846, in connection
with a commission from the Birmingham Music Festival in England. Depicting or reflecting

on events in the life of the prophet Elijah, the texts are taken mainly from the first book of Kings in the Old Testament, but also incorporate other biblical passages, especially from the Psalms. The original German libretto was fashioned by Mendelssohn's collaborator on *St. Paul*, the Rev. Julius Schubring; for the premiere it was translated into English by William Bartholomew, with the composer's active collaboration.

Elijah is modeled on the oratorios of Handel and the passions of Bach. The story of the prophet's suffering and redemption is divided into two parts and told in a dramatic succession of solo, ensembles, and choral numbers. There are moments of blazing passion and of gentle meditation. The chorus "He, watching over Israel" is of the latter type. It comes in Part 2 of the oratorio, when Elijah, sleeping under a juniper tree, is protected by angels from the wrath of the Israelites, who see him as challenging the power of King Ahab and his queen Jezebel.

Mendelssohn's musical language in this chorus exemplifies his strongly classicizing type of Romanticism. It is expressive without exaggeration, harmonically rich without ever becoming really dissonant or chromatic. In the orchestra, Mendelssohn provides a gently rocking accompaniment in triplets that continues throughout almost the entire four-minute chorus, creating a lullaby that seems to cradle the prophet. The number divides roughly into a ternary design, as determined by the thematic material, the harmonic plan, and the presentation of the text: **A** (mm. 1–19), **B** (mm. 19–43), **A′** (mm. 43–66), **coda** (mm. 67–79). The first part (mm. 1–19) is primarily in D major and uses the text from Psalm 121 ("He, watching over Israel . . ."). It is diatonic and is dominated by a simple but memorable theme introduced by the sopranos and taken up successively by the different voices in rich polyphony, but not in a fugal manner.

The cadence to D in measure 19 marks the end of the first psalm verse. A strong contrast emerges for the beginning of the text from Psalm 38 ("Shouldst thou, walking in grief, languish.") In a manner and mood appropriate to the words, a new theme is introduced and treated in strict fugal style, and the music becomes more chromatic and unstable, moving to the key area of iii or F♯ minor. In measure 43, Mendelssohn moves to an open half cadence on V of F♯ minor, or C♯ major. At this point he subtly prepares a return to the opening theme, which appears in the sopranos at its original pitch (m. 44), but is initially harmonized by a fleeting iii chord carried over from the **B** section. Only at measure 47 does the tonic D arrive, confirming the return.

The return (**A′**) is greatly modified, not only by the harmony, but also because the **B** theme continues to be heard, now combined ingeniously with the **A** theme. From measure 51 on, **B** disappears, as the "grief" and "anguish" give way definitively to the serene mood and text of **A**. A strong cadence to D occurs at measure 59, and in the next measure Mendelssohn inflects the tonic chord with a C-natural, thus turning it into a dominant seventh that tilts toward the subdominant, which is touched on in measure 65. Such a harmonic gesture indicates the movement is approaching its close. After the next cadence to the tonic (m. 67), a coda begins over a sustained D pedal. In measures 71–77, for the first time in this movement, the chorus sings a cappella, without accompaniment. It is a kind of cadenza for the chorus, which brings the dynamic level down to a hushed *pianissimo* before the orchestra reenters for a final three measures of pure tonic harmony.

Mendelssohn's chorus thus traces a broad arc, starting from and returning to a mood of comfort, passing in between through turbulence and instability. The musical structure is perfectly calibrated to the emotional and spiritual design.

HECTOR BERLIOZ (1803–1869)

Symphonie fantastique: Movement 2, *Un bal*
Program symphony, 1830

From Hector Berlioz, *Symphonie Fantastique and Harold in Italy.* New York: Dover Publications, Inc.

269

342

358

The artist finds himself in the most varied situations—in the midst of *the tumult of a party*, in the peaceful contemplation of the beauties of nature; but everywhere, in the town, in the country, the beloved image appears before him and disturbs his peace of mind.
—*from Berlioz's program*

Berlioz's *Symphonie fantastique* is the most famous piece of program music of the nineteenth century, and one of the earliest. Berlioz provided a scenario or "program" (his own term) to be distributed to audiences when the symphony was performed. The program is thus an integral part of the work, or at least of how the composer wanted it to be experienced. Berlioz well knew that music and words have different expressive capacities. The program would, he said, not duplicate but rather "fill the gaps" in the musical discourse, which he felt was inevitably less precise than text.

The program of the *Symphonie fantastique* traces the obsession of a "young musician" with a woman whom he pursues but never attains. Neither he nor she is named, but it is well documented that Berlioz based the program on his own real-life infatuation with an Irish actress, Harriet Smithson. In the symphony, the beloved is depicted by a recurring theme, called by Berlioz an *idée fixe* (fixed idea or fixation), a term that captures the obsessive nature of this attachment. The *idée fixe* appears in all five movements, transformed each time according to the musical context and the program.

The second movement of the *Symphonie fantastique* fulfills the role of the "dance" movement—usually a minuet or scherzo—in the standard symphony. Berlioz's program is less explicit here than elsewhere: all he mentions is a "party." But the movement's title in the score ("Un bal") and initial tempo-mood indication ("Valse") are unambiguous. The waltz had been developed as an elegant but vigorous ballroom dance in the later eighteenth century. While it made sporadic appearances in concert music, Berlioz may have been the first composer to include it in a symphony, at least in such a prominent way.

Like a symphonic minuet or scherzo, *Un bal* has a ternary structure, which Berlioz frames with an introduction and extended coda, and into which he nests further ternary forms:

FORM	Introduction	A			B	A′			Coda
SUBSECTION		a	b	c	[*idée fixe*]	a	b	c	[*idée fixe*]
MEASURE	1	36	56	94	121	176	193	233	256

The introduction, where one can imagine the dancers arriving, pairing up, and assuming their positions, avoids any distinct waltz rhythm. Instead, Berlioz uses his orchestral magic to conjure an ambiguous cloud of sonorities—tremolos in the upper strings, and upward sweeping arpeggios in the cellos, double basses, and harps. The prominence of the harps at the opening and in the waltz sections is unusual in a symphonic piece of the period. The harmony wanders upward chromatically and by sequence, and not until measure 30 do we get a sense of the eventual tonic, A major. When the waltz at last emerges after three measures of robust "oom-pah-pah" accompaniment (mm. 36–38), it features a swirling violin melody that seems to capture the physical motion of the dance. The momentary slowing up or rallentando at the end of the third phrase (mm. 49–50), followed by the return to the main tempo, is Berlioz's subtle homage to the Viennese tradition of the waltz (see Chapter 3).

If the symphony's protagonist is participating in this waltz, he seems at this point to have few worries. But, as the program tells us, his peace of mind never lasts long. The beloved appears and—at least in the mind of the protagonist—interrupts the waltz, initiating the **B** segment of the movement, which is analogous to the trio, a middle contrasting dance, but here is also an integral part of the programmatic and musical continuity. At first, as if to reflect the surprise generated by the beloved's arrival, the waltz accompaniment stops altogether (m. 116). A spotlight is thrown on the beloved by the suddenly reduced dynamics and thinned-out orchestration. The *idée fixe* now appears (m. 120) in the flute and oboe in the key of F, a major third below the tonic (a favorite harmonic relationship of the Romantics). It is accompanied in the cellos and double basses by the throbbing staccato figure (perhaps a heart beat?) that was also part of the original presentation of the *idée fixe* in the first movement. As her melody assumes momentum and the beloved begins to dance, the circular figuration of the original waltz reappears in the strings.

A transition leads from F major back to the dominant of A, and the waltz returns (**A'**), now with the accompaniment and orchestration enhanced, and the theme extended. Has the protagonist managed at last to banish thoughts of the beloved? The long coda tells us otherwise. At first the waltz seems to be building inexorably toward a climax, with an increase in tempo and dynamics. Then it breaks off abruptly (m. 302), and the *idée fixe* appears plaintively and *pianissimo* in the solo clarinet, accompanied only by horns and a brief arpeggio in the harps. But the beloved in turn is herself interrupted by an almost violent return of the full orchestra (m. 320). The waltz now sweeps toward a conclusion that seems giddy but not triumphant. The composer-protagonist cannot erase the disturbing emotions called up by the *idée fixe*, which (or who) will continue to haunt him across the symphony.

Années de pèlerinage I, Suisse: No. 4, Au bord d'une source
1855

From Franz Liszt, Années de Pèlerinage, Complete. New York: Dover Publications, Inc.

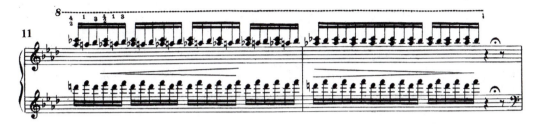

*) Possible variant fingering:

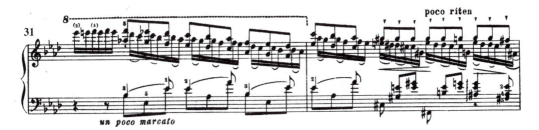

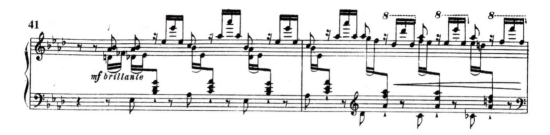

Inspired by landscapes he visited on his travels around Europe, Liszt created some of the greatest tone paintings for piano of the nineteenth century, including those collected in three sets of pieces he called *Années de pèlerinage* (Years of Pilgrimage, sometimes also translated as Years of Wandering). *Au bord d'une source* (Beside a spring) appears in the first volume of *Années*, which is subtitled *Suisse* (Switzerland). Liszt prefaces the piece with an engraving showing a goatherd and his flock relaxing and refreshing themselves at an idyllic spot where a mountain spring flows into a small river (see Chapter 6, Fig. 6.2). Inscribed on the image are verses by the German poet Friedrich Schiller, which read: "In murmuring coolness begin the games of young nature."

Liszt's four-minute piece is a musical portrait of rippling water, ingeniously realized for the piano and demanding the highest level of technical proficiency. The thematic kernel of *Au bord* is:

The example represents how the theme sounds to the ear. But it does not appear on the page in this form; rather, as can be seen from the score, it is always divided between the hands, which cross continually in a texture that is refracted across the entire range of the piano. This process of refraction is as much the "theme" as are the actual notes of the melody.

The structure of *Au bord* seems literally to flow from the repetition and variation of the initial material, whose appearances are separated by brief cadenza-like interludes. The formal plan can be rendered as:

A' + cadenza-interlude (mm. 1–12)

A' + cadenza-interlude (mm. 13–27)

A'' + cadenza-interlude (mm. 28–40)

A''' + cadenza-interlude (mm. 41–50)

Coda: built from **A** + cadenza (mm. 51–67)

Such letter names are, however, somewhat misleading because Liszt seems not to have been writing with a traditional strophic or variation form in mind. *Au bord d'une source* is really generated by a constant reworking of color and texture, for which the **A** theme is a vehicle.

Liszt's harmonic language is equally remarkable and nontraditional. The piece is in the key of A♭ but rarely settles into that key until the end. Liszt frequently shifts, without real modulation, into other remote keys, and he sometimes—especially in the cadenza-interludes—hovers in a kind of chromatic netherworld that has no specific key at all. The tonal fluidity is apparent from the start, when the key or key area slips from A♭ to B major (m. 5), then to B♭ (m. 7), which is sustained through the cadenza-interlude, and then reinterpreted, after the fermata of measure 12, as V of V of the tonic A♭, which returns as **A'** begins (m. 13).

As apparent in the **A'** segment, harmonic relationships by thirds, characteristic of the Romantic era, often replace or supplement traditional dominant–tonic relationships. The principal secondary key in *Au bord*, appearing on several occasions, is E major, which lies a major third below the tonic. At measure 13, Liszt begins the theme in the tonic A♭, but on the third beat of measure 16 slips to the dominant of E major, a B dominant seventh chord, which then resolves to E major at measure 17. Two measures later (m. 19) the E drops a half step to E♭, the dominant of A♭, which is sustained or prolonged until the end of the cadenza-interlude (downbeat of m. 28).

The fluid harmonic language of *Au bord* fully supports the thematic language and the treatment of the piano texture. All these structural and expressive elements work together to create a magnificent image in sound of water flowing from the spring. Indeed, the effect is almost tactile for both performer and listener. The links between music, the visual, and the sensuous have never been explored more effectively than in Liszt's piano works, especially in a piece like *Au bord d'une source*.

Nocturne in B♭ Minor, Op. 9, No. 1

Nocturne (character piece), 1830–32

From Frédéric Chopin, *Nocturnes and Polonaises.* New York: Dover Publications, Inc.

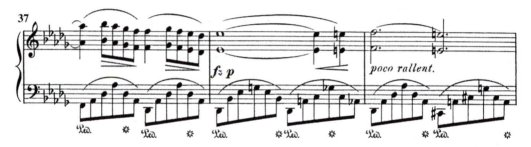

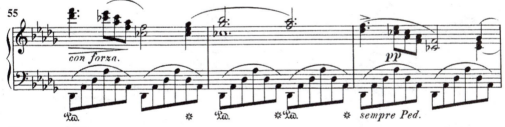

Chopin composed 21 nocturnes, of which 18 were published in his lifetime, in sets of two or three. Among the most beloved and frequently performed of his works, the nocturnes exemplify many aspects of Chopin's approach to the shorter lyrical piano piece. Though the title "nocturne" has no exact definition, it can be thought of as a "night piece" or serenade. The Irish composer John Field (1782–1837) had developed the piano nocturne earlier in the nineteenth century. Chopin, who knew and admired Field's works, greatly expanded the technical and expressive dimensions of the genre, bringing to bear his own special genius for chromatic harmony, limpid melody, and contrapuntal richness.

The B♭-Minor Nocturne, from Chopin's first set of three, Op. 9, was composed between 1830 and 1832. It was dedicated to the pianist Camille Pleyel, the daughter-in-law of the renowned publisher and piano maker Ignace Pleyel. Chopin's nocturne differs from forms like the sonata in that it lacks ongoing or continuous development of themes. On the largest scale, the B♭-Minor Nocturne has a clearly articulated ternary form (**ABA′**), which is distinctive here because the central section is considerably longer than the flanking ones. In turn, each section divides into regular phrases of mostly four and eight measures. As in Liszt's *Au bord d'une source* (Anthology 8), there is considerable repetition, and minimal variation of thematic material. The piece is in a real sense "about" the constant ornamentation of themes.

A conventional way of writing the **a** phrase might place the opening melodic flourish on a downbeat and support it with a tonic harmony. Instead, Chopin makes the gesture a long unaccompanied upbeat. The tonic chord arrives only with the downbeat of measure 1, where the melody has already moved on to the dominant pitch F. This metrical and harmonic ambiguity persists throughout the **A** section. In measure 4 and again in measure 13, the repeated B♭s, which recall the Fs from measure 1, are now placed in the weak half of the measure. Chopin "rights" the metrical grid with the **B** theme, which begins firmly on the notated downbeat and proceeds in two-measure units. For the sake of convenience, in the formal chart of the nocturne we have identified the beginnings of the thematic units within **A** as the measure where the downbeat arrives, although this representation belies the fluid aural experience.

SECTION	A				B									A′		
THEME	a	b	a′	codetta	c	c′	c	c′	d	c′	d	c′	codetta	a	codetta	coda
KEY	B♭ minor				D♭ major									B♭ minor-major		
MEASURE	1	5	9	13	19	23	27	31	35	39	43	47	51	71	75	81

Ornamentation is integral to the melodic style of the nocturne. Even at its first repetition (mm. 2–3) the melody is decorated. The six-note upbeat figure is embellished into an 11-note roulade, and the simple repeated Fs become a chromatic wash of 22 small notes. In Chopin, as in Bellini, it is a mistake to distinguish "theme" from "ornament" because the two are intimately linked.

The texture of this nocturne is characteristic of the genre. A broad arpeggiated accompaniment in the left hand underpins a lyrical melody that has a simple basic skeleton ornamented by cascades of smaller notes. This texture remains consistent throughout the nocturne. Chopin modeled this style on the long cantilena melodies of Italian opera, as in Bellini's *Casta diva* from *Norma* (Anthology 3).

The nocturne has a clear tonal plan. The **A** section is primarily in B♭ minor, the large **B** section in the relative major, D♭ major. The **A′** section ends in B♭ major. Within these broad harmonic areas, Chopin makes frequent harmonic shifts or modulations. The **A** section first moves toward the relative major, D♭, which is inflected by its own minor subdominant, G♭ minor (m. 6). This chord incorporates the note B♭♭, which is enharmonically A♮. Chopin is "marking" this note for later expansion in the **B** section, where the actual harmony of A major appears (m. 23) as part of a major enharmonic shift, which includes respelling F♭ as E♮. The A major becomes V of D major, which arrives in measure 24. We thus find ourselves in a key lying a half step above the main key of the **B** section, D♭. This is one of the most remote harmonic relationships available to Chopin. Yet D vanishes almost as soon as it appears. A diminished seventh chord on the second half of measure 25 leads us back to D♭ major.

The closing segment or codetta of the **B** section is long, comprising almost a quarter of the whole nocturne, from measure 51 to the return of **A′** at measure 71. Chopin lingers over the D♭ harmony, which first appears with its flatted seventh, then without. The codetta is remarkable for its stasis, its floating quality unlike anything we would hear in a pre-Romantic work.

With the return to B♭ minor for **A′** we would expect a B♭ in the bass. But Chopin carries over the D♭ bass from the **B** section, and the tonic chord in the second half of measure 70 appears in first inversion. Only on the next downbeat does the chord arrive in root position, with a B♭ in the bass.

Dichterliebe, Op. 48: *Im wunderschönen Monat Mai* and *Aus meinen Tränen sprießen*

Lieder (song cycle), 1840

1. *Im wunderschönen Monat Mai*

From Robert Schumann, *Selected Songs for Solo Voice and Piano*. New York: Dover.

2. *Aus meinen Tränen sprießen*

1.

Im wunderschönen Monat Mai,	*In the wonderful month of May,*
Als alle Knospen sprangen,	*When all the buds came out,*
Da ist in meinem Herzen	*Then in my heart*
Die Liebe aufgegangen.	*Love burst forth.*
Im wunderschönen Monat Mai,	*In the wonderful month of May,*
Als alle Vögel sangen,	*When all the birds were singing,*
Da hab' ich ihr gestanden	*Then I confessed to her*
Mein Sehnen und Verlangen.	*My yearning and longing.*

2.

Aus meinen Tränen sprießen	*From my tears sprout forth*
Viel blühende Blumen hervor,	*Many blooming flowers,*
Und meine Seufzer werden	*And my sighing becomes*
Ein Nachtigallenchor.	*A choir of nightingales.*
Und wenn du mich lieb hast, Kindchen,	*And if you love me, little one,*
Schenk' ich dir die Blumen all',	*I'll give you all the flowers,*
Und vor deinem Fenster soll klingen	*And before your window will sound*
Das Lied der Nachtigall.	*The song of the nightingale.*

—Heinrich Heine

Robert Schumann wrote his song cycle *Dichterliebe* (A Poet's Love) in the spring of 1840. He would call 1840 his *Liederjahr* or year of song, because it saw the composition of 120 lieder, almost half his total output in that genre. Most of the songs were inspired by his love for Clara Wieck, whom Schumann was finally able to marry in September, overcoming the objections and legal maneuvers of her father, Friedrich Wieck.

    Dichterliebe comprises settings of sixteen texts from the collection *Lyrisches Intermezzo* by the prominent German Romantic poet Heinrich Heine. Schumann arranged the poems to suggest but not specify a narrative of unrequited love; the cycle is really a series of psychological self-portraits of a lovelorn poet. The emotional states range widely, from longing, to anticipation, to pleading, to jealousy, to anger, and finally to grim resignation, when at the end the poet decides to toss his sorrows into the Rhine River. Irony is a strong component of Heine's poems, which sometimes seem to say one thing (usually positive) while really meaning another (negative).

    In the opening songs of *Dichterliebe* the poet is still in an optimistic frame of mind. The first, dominated by images of spring, is all about anticipation, as he confesses longing and desire for his beloved. In the second song, he is already shedding tears, but they are tears of hope, watering the flowers he will offer his beloved. Only in the seventh poem of the cycle do things turn darker and bitterer.

Like many poems in *Dichterliebe* (and in German Romantic song in general), the first two are dominated by images of nature. But nowhere in the cycle does Schumann aim to depict these in the piano, as Schubert (Anthology 2) and other composers of an earlier generation so often did. There is no flowing figuration to depict the Rhine River, which is mentioned in several poems. Rather, it is the mood, the emotions, that Schumann translates into music. Throughout the first song, with its unfulfilled longing, we are uncertain whether the key is F♯ minor or A major. The opening progression seems to suggest iv^6–V^7 in F♯ minor, but that key is never reached. The B-minor chord that functions as iv in F♯ minor is reinterpreted as ii in A major, and it is to that key that Schumann cadences in measure 6. The ending of song 1 on a sustained C♯ dominant seventh chord perpetuates the ambiguity, which carries over into song 2 of the cycle. Song 2 begins with an A–C♯ dyad that could represent either the third and fifth degrees of F♯ minor or the first and third of A major. Within a few measures, Schumann resolves the ambiguity with two firm cadences to A major (mm. 3–4).

In addition to harmonic ambiguity, Schumann communicates longing through frequent suspensions, suppressed downbeats in some parts of the texture, and an intricate piano style in which inner voices seem to come and go freely. Song 1 begins with a sixteenth-note upbeat, C♯, which is tied over the barline and sustained into the second half of the measure before it resolves down to B, thus creating a long 7–6 suspension above the bass D. Such techniques create strong dissonance and give the accompaniment an irregular, halting quality.

In *Dichterliebe* Schumann cultivates a special relationship between piano and voice. In songs 1 and 2, the top line of the piano does not so much double as "shadow" the voice part. In measure 9 of song 1, the piano's melodic notes B and C♯ arrive after the voice, on the weak sixteenth notes. On the downbeat of the next measure, at "Herzen," and then two measures later at "-gangen," the voice breaks free from the piano, reaching up to create a climax. Elsewhere, the voice seems to end phrases in midstream or midthought, and the piano continues the thread, as happens at the end of song 1 ("Verlangen," mm. 22–23) or in song 2 ("hervor," mm. 3–4). The piano functions somewhat like the unconscious of the poet/singer; or perhaps it is another "character," commenting on the protagonist's situation. In song 2, indeed, it is the piano that takes over, after hesitant fermatas, to make the definitive cadence to A major in measures 4, 8, and 16–17. As often happens in *Dichterliebe,* the piano accomplishes what the voice cannot or will not do on its own.

HUGO WOLF (1860–1903)

Mörike-Lieder: **No. 24**, *In der Frühe*

Lied, 1888

From Hugo Wolf, *The Complete Mörike Songs*. New York: Dover Publications, Inc.

Zwei-feln her und hin und schaf-fet Nacht - ge-spen - ster.

(innig und zart)

_Äng - ste, quä - le dich nicht län - ger, mei - ne See - le!

Freu' dich! Schon sind da und dor - ten

Mor - gen - glo - cken wach _____ ge-

Kein Schlaf noch kühlt das Auge mir,	*No sleep has yet cooled my eyes,*
Dort gehet schon der Tag herfür	*Day is already beginning to appear*
An meinem Kammerfenster.	*At the window of my bedroom.*
Es wühlet mein verstörter Sinn	*My disturbed spirit is still buffeted about*
Noch zwischen Zweifeln her und hin	*Back and forth between doubts*
Und schaffet Nachtgespenster.	*And creates nocturnal ghosts.*
—Ängste, quäle	*—Do not frighten and torture*
Dich nicht länger, meine Seele!	*Yourself any longer, my soul!*
Freu' dich! Schon sind da und dorten	*Rejoice! Already here and there*
Morgenglocken wach geworden.	*Morning bells have awakened.*

—Eduard Mörike

Hugo Wolf focused almost his entire compositional efforts on lieder; he composed more than 300 between the mid-1870s and 1897. His most intense creative period, between 1888 and 1891, includes the 53 songs set to texts by the early Romantic poet Eduard Mörike (1804–1875). Wolf's songs are distinctive for his meticulous attention to poetic declamation and for the dense chromaticism of his harmonic language. Although Wolf was certainly influenced by Richard Wagner in both respects, he forged a musical style very much his own.

Wolf felt that lieder should above all respect the literary qualities of poetry. His title for the Mörike collection reflects this priority. In English it reads "Poems by Eduard Mörike for voice and piano composed . . . by Hugo Wolf." Wolf uses the term *Gedichte* (poems), avoiding the terms *Lieder* or *Gesänge* that other composers commonly employ. And the poet's name takes precedence over the composer's, which comes only at the end of the title. Such humility did not mean, however, that Wolf restricted himself to a minimal musical setting. Rather, the music is put fully in the service of the poem to create something greater than the sum of the parts.

Mörike's poem *In der Frühe* (Early Morning) is written in the person of an anguished soul who has just had a sleepless night but finds hope in the sound of morning bells—presumably tolling in some local church. The poem has ten lines, of which the first six form a pair of three-line units. Each unit has the rhyme scheme *aab* and an iambic meter (short-long), in which the *a* lines have eight syllables and the *b* lines have seven. The shorter seventh line breaks the pattern abruptly, with four syllables in trochaic meter (long-short) and a stark image of despair. The poem turns to the more positive images for the final three lines. Line 8 both completes the thought of line 7—the "nicht" negates the verbs of the preceding line—and forms part of a final three-line unit, with eight syllables per line. But the unit is different than in lines 1–6: the trochaic meter established in the shorter seventh line continues to govern, and the rhyme scheme is changed to *abb*.

Wolf divides his setting of the poem into two large sections corresponding to the two principal moods of the text. The first (mm. 1–10) is in minor, the second (mm. 11–22) in major. As in the poem, line 7 is the musical turning point. In the first part, Wolf's setting closely resembles speech rhythm—the way the text would be spoken. As befits the grammar and sense of words (dawn appearing at the window), Wolf runs together lines 2 and 3 (mm. 3–4) in a continuous musical phrase. But there is also musical symmetry. The contour of the three-note unit at the opening of the second phrase ("Es wühlet," m. 6) matches that in measure 1, as does the cadence of a descending fifth at the end (compare "fenster" in m. 4 and "-spenster" in m. 9). In the second half of the song, the vocal expression becomes much more vivid and expansive. The last two lines of the poem occupy nine measures. Wolf emphasizes the new trochaic patterns of lines with extended notes on the long syllables ("Ang-," "Freu'," "Mor-," etc.), usually followed by large melodic leaps.

The relationship between piano and voice in Wolf's song is very different from that in Schumann's *Im wunderschönen Monat Mai* (Anthology 10), where the piano part tends to shadow and sometimes double the voice. Wolf's piano has a more independent musical identity, built from a striking, somber one-measure thematic unit (m. 1). The song's entire material is generated from two motivic components, a neighbor-note figure and a rising third, presented in a five-note rhythmic pattern that is repeated again and again. In the first half, the piano part is shaped into two five-measure segments that underpin the two three-line poetic units. The second half of the song (from m. 11) features sequential repetition of the theme or its rising-third motive.

The real motion in *In der Frühe* is generated by the harmonic activity in the piano. The larger trajectory is conventional: a dark D minor leading to a radiant D major. But that journey is articulated at the local level by bold harmonic shifts that elide standard dominant–tonic relationships. The first five-measure unit moves from the tonic D minor to a remote B major. We might expect this B to function as V of V (E) of V (A). But the next five-measure unit begins directly on A minor (m. 6), thus bypassing resolution from the dominant E. A transitional measure (m. 10) concludes with a chord spelled as an altered ("German") sixth within E major (C–E–G–A♯). But as occurred in mm. 5–6, the expected harmonic resolution is elided; there is no standard dominant, and the German sixth resolves directly to E major in m. 11. Now the piano unfolds an extraordinary series of modulations upward by thirds, from E (m. 11), to G (m. 14), and B♭ (m. 16), settling at last on the tonic major D (m. 18).

The poet's initial sense of being trapped is conveyed by the highly restricted motivic-thematic process and the repeated patterns in the piano in measures 1 to 10. The sense of release comes in the second part, measures 11 to 22, when those same patterns are liberated by the rising harmonic sequences. As he has done in reaching principal harmonic goals earlier in the song, Wolf avoids traditional dominant relationships. It is a tribute to his mastery that the final D major sounds so convincing and inevitable.

Boris Godunov: Act 2, Boris's monologue

Opera, 1872

From Modest Musorgsky, *Boris Godunov*. Wiesbaden: Breitkopf & Härtel.

17 (спокойно)

На _ прас _ но мнѣ ку _ дес _ ни _ ки су _ лятъ Дни дол _ гі _ е, дни вла _ сти

23 (оживленно)

без _ мя _ теж _ ной Ни жизнь, ни власть, ни сла _ вы о _ боль _

29

щень _ я, Ни кли _ ки тол _ пы, ме _ ня __ не ве _ се _ лятъ!

36 (спокойно)

Въ семь _ ѣ сво _ ей я мнилъ най _ ти от _ ра _ ду, Го _ то _ вилъ до _ че _ ри ве _

(lebhaft)

крестъ лишь тьма и мракъ непроглядный!   Хо_тя мелькнуль бы лучъ от_ра _ ды!

cresc.

И   скор_бью   сер_дце пол_но, То_ску_етъ, то_мит_ся   духъ у_сталый.

pp

Ка_кой то тре_петъ тайный... все ждешь че_го_то...   Мо_

pp

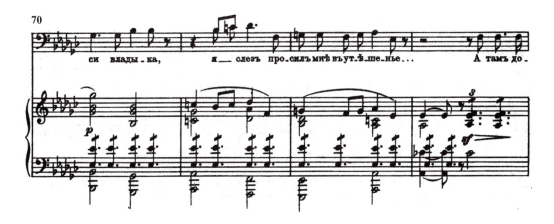

74

носъ: бо_яръ кра_мо_ла,   Коз_ни Лит_вы   и тай_ны_е под_ко_пы, Гладъ и

78

моръ,   и трусъ и раз_зо_ре   нье. Сло_вно ди_кiй звѣрь ры_щетъ людъ за_чу_

81
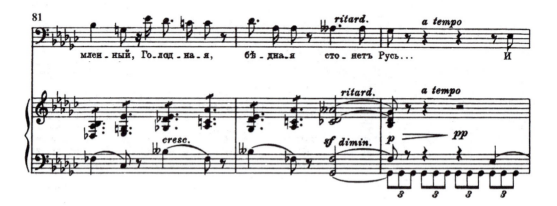

млен_ный, Го_лод_на_я,   бѣ_дна_я   сто_нетъ Русь...   И

въ лю _ томъ го _ рѣ, ни_спо_слан_номъ Бо _ гомъ, За тяж_кiй нашъ грѣхъвъис_пы_

та _ нье, Ви _ ной всѣхъ золъ ме _ ня на_ре_ка_ютъ,Кля_

нутъ на площадяхъ и _ мя Бо_ри_са! И да_же

сонъ бѣжитъ, и въ сум-ра-кѣ но-чи Дитя о - кро - ва -

влен - но-е встаетъ... О-чи пы-ла - ютъ, стиснувъ ру-чон - ки,

про-ситъ по-ща - ды... И не бы-ло по-ща-ды! Страш-на-я ра-на зі -

я - етъ! Слы - шится крикъ е - го пред-смертный... О Гос-по-ди Бо-же-мой!

BORIS

I have achieved supreme power.	Достиг я высшей власти.
It is already the sixth year that I reign in peace	Шестой уж год я царствую спокойно,
(animated)	*(оживленно)*
But there is no happiness in my tormented soul.	Но счастья нет моей измученной душе.
(quiet)	*(спокойно)*
In vain the soothsayers promise me A long life and many days of untroubled power.	Напрасно мне кудесники сулят Дни долгие, дни власти безмятежной.
(animated)	*(оживленно)*
Neither life, nor power, not the vanities of glory,	Ни жизнь, ни власть, ни славы обольщенья,
Not the jubilation of the crowd give me joy!	Ни клики толпы меня не веселят!
(quiet)	*(спокойно)*
In my family I imagined I would find happiness,	В семье своей я мнил найти отраду,
I was preparing a joyous wedding feast for my daughter,	Готовил дочери веселый брачный пир,
My tsarevna, the innocent dove.	Моей царевне, голубке чистой.
(animated)	*(оживленно)*
Like a storm, death carried off the bridegroom!	Как буря, смерть уносит жениха!
(lost in thought)	*(задумавшись)*
How heavily weighs the arm of the awesome judge,	Тяжка десница грозного судии,
How terrible his sentence on the criminal soul . . .	Ужасен приговор душе преступной. . .
All around me is but darkness and impenetrable gloom!	Окрест лишь тьма и мрак непроглядный!
If there were a single ray of comfort!	Хотя мелькнул бы луч отрады!
My heart is full of sorrow,	И скорбью сердце полно,
It languishes under the weight of weary thoughts.	Волнуясь, томится дух усталый.

(in a whisper)	*(шопотом)*
A secret trepidation . . . One always awaits something . . .	Какой-то трепет тайный... Все ждешь чего-то...
With a fervent prayer to the Lord's saints	Молитвой тёплой к угодникам Божьим
I imagined that I could mute the suffering of my soul . . .	Я мнил заглушить души страданья...
Amid all grandeur and splendor of unlimited power,	В величьи и блеске власти безграничной,
The sovereign of all Russia, all I begged for were tears of solace! . . .	Руси владыка, я слёз просил мне в утешенье!....
But then—a report: the sedition of the boyars,	А там донос: бояр крамола,
The intrigues of Lithuania, and secret conspiracies.	Козни Литвы и тайные подкопы,
Hunger, pestilence, earthquakes, and devastation . . .	Глад, и мор, и трус, и разоренье...
Like a wild beast, our plague-ridden people roam about;	Словно дикий зверь, рыщет люд зачумленный;
Starving, impoverished, Russia is groaning . . .	Голодная, бедная, стонет Русь...
And in this dire sorrow, sent by God	И в лютом горе, ниспосланном Богом
As a trial for our grievous sin,	За тяжкий наш грех в испытанье,
They name me the cause of all calamities,	Виной всех зол меня нарекают,
Cursing the name of Boris on the squares!	Клянут на площадях имя Бориса!
Even sleep eludes me, and in the darkness of night	И даже сон бежит, и в сумраке ночи
The child appears in front of me, covered with blood. . . .	Дитя окровавленное встает...
His eyes blaze, and clenching his little arms,	Очи пылают, стиснув ручёнки,
He begs for mercy . . . But there was no mercy!	Просит пощады... И не было пощады!
The terrible wound gapes wide! The sound of his mortal cry is in the air . . .	Страшная рана зияет! Слышится крик его предсмертный...
(Jumps up and sinks heavily into the chair)	*(Вскакивает и тяжело опускается в кресло)*
O, Lord, o my God. . . .	О Господи, Боже мой. . . .

—Alexander Pushkin, with additions by Musorgsky; translation by Boris Gasparov.

Musorgsky fashioned his own libretto for *Boris Godunov* from a historical tragedy by Alexander Pushkin about the turbulent reign of the tsar Boris, who ascended to the Russian throne in 1598 and died in 1605. It was claimed in Boris's day that he had ordered the murder of the three-year-old Dmitri, a son of Ivan the Terrible and possible pretender to the throne. Although today scholars believe Boris was probably not responsible for the crime, in Pushkin's play and Musorgsky's opera his guilt is assumed and indeed propels the action.

Musorgsky completed the first version of *Boris Godunov* in 1869. After it was rejected by the Directorate of Imperial Theaters in St. Petersburg for lacking a leading female role, he rewrote the opera, adding the character of Marina and a new act (Act 3) in which she appears. The revision was finished in 1872 and had its premiere in 1874.

Boris Godunov is at once a political drama, played out on a broad scale with choruses and crowd scenes, and an interior drama, played out in the mind and soul of the main character, who is one of the great creations of nineteenth-century opera. The Act 2 soliloquy for Boris is our first extended look in the opera into his complex, conflicted personality. A striking early example of what in literature and psychology would later be characterized as stream of consciousness, the number is characteristic of the naturalism toward which Musorgsky strove in *Boris*. In the original version of 1869, the composer had taken over Pushkin's prose-like text almost word for word and had set it in a style close to melodic recitative. In the 1872 revision, as it appears in this anthology, Musorgsky made many changes to the text and gave the vocal part more expansive lyricism (in part by adapting some music composed for an earlier, incomplete opera, *Salammbô*). He also divided the number more clearly into what might be recognized as recitative and aria, the latter beginning at the Andante (m. 47) with the change of tempo, key signature, and meter, and the appearance of a broad melody that is repeated several times.

Boris begins by wondering why his royal power and his loving family do not bring him contentment. Then the litany of sorrows and concerns begin to pour out: first the tragic death of his daughter's fiancé, then the disloyalties of the noblemen (boyars) and the natural disasters and famines that have visited the Russian people. Finally Boris is visited by the image that terrifies him most—the child Dmitri, whom he has had murdered.

Musorgsky shapes the music to mirror Boris's changing frame of mind. One basic technique is that of the Wagnerian leitmotif, a theme associated with a specific character or idea. While in Wagner's operas leitmotifs appear mainly in the orchestra, in *Boris Godunov* they often appear in the vocal parts as well. When Boris sings of the prediction of a long reign (m. 16), we hear a lyrical theme, beginning *pianissimo* and in A major, associated with his majesty and power. The mention of his daughter Xenia (m. 36) ushers in her gentle theme in A♭ major. At the end (m. 73), the chromatic descending triplets symbolic of Boris's guilt accompany his haunting vision of Dmitri.

Musorgsky's innovative harmonic language, also following closely the character's mood, ranges from broad diatonicism to destabilizing chromaticism. At the opening of the monologue, Boris sings about his political power to triadic harmonies oriented around G♯ minor. The aria-like section at measure 47 is oriented around G♭ major and E♭ minor. Its tonal language becomes increasingly dissonant with Boris's mounting agitation. Beginning at measure 73, in a striking harmonic progression, Musorgsky alternates two dissonances, half-diminished seventh chords and augmented triads. First they alternate once per measure, then twice. The final segment of the monologue (from m. 92) is dominated by slithering, disorienting chromatic scales that are anchored but not really rationalized by a pedal E♭. Especially when sustained over many measures, effects like the alternating dissonances or chromatic scales undermine any clear tonal center and demonstrate why Musorgsky's musical language could exert such a powerful influence on composers of early Modernism, including Stravinsky and Debussy.

The recordings of Boris's monologue downloadable from iTunes and Amazon via StudySpace correspond exactly to the vocal score in this anthology, which reproduces Musorgsky's version of 1872. Many other recordings of the opera, especially those made before the last decades of the twentieth century—and including those available on Naxos via StudySpace—use the version of the score prepared in 1896 by Nikolay Rimsky-Korsakov (a fellow member, with Musorgsky, of the so-called Mighty Handful of Russian composers). Rimsky felt that that Musorgsky's opera was too thinly and amateurishly orchestrated, and he lavished his skills particularly upon that dimension of the score. In Boris's monologue, Rimsky also regularized the notated meter in the opening recitative segment and transposed the first five measures of the aria-like portion up a fourth, with some adjustments in the voice part.

Piano Trio No. 4 (*Dumky*), Op. 90: Movement 6

Piano trio, 1891

From Antonín Dvořák, *Chamber Music for Piano and Strings.* New York: Dover Publications, Inc.

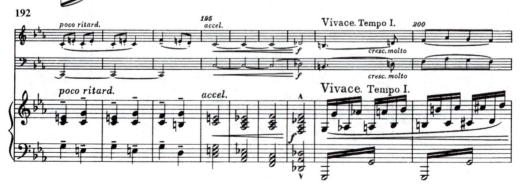

Dvořák provided his last piano trio with the subtitle *Dumky*, the plural form of a Slavic (originally Ukranian) name for a vocal or instrumental folk piece that is ruminative or melancholic in character and proceeds in alternating sections of slow and fast tempos. Unique in the Classical–Romantic tradition of chamber music, Dvořák's trio comprises a suite of six relatively short *dumka* movements, each in a different key. The *Dumky* Trio exemplifies Dvořák's remarkable ability to capture sonorities he associated with the Czech people of his native Bohemia, and then fold them into the forms and techniques of the high art traditions of music.

Dvořák's instrumental writing often seems to evoke the sparse textures of folk music more than the robust sonorities of Romantic chamber music. The piano part is unusually lean at the opening: in measures 1–2 the theme consists of a single line doubled between the hands; in measures 9–11, the right and left hand alternate solo passages. The cello often lies very high in its range (as in measures 17–22 and most of the subsequent Vivace), while the violin frequently occupies a low register (m. 23ff.).

The folklike features of the movement also include frequent repetition of motives and themes (as opposed to more conventional development), pedal points or drones (as opposed to directed harmonic progressions), ostinato-like figures, and modal-sounding scales and harmonies. Especially characteristic is the appearance of the Neapolitan degree D♭ in the context of C major (as in mm. 119–31), with repeated emphasis on the interval of the augmented second (D♭–E♮), a common feature of Eastern European folk musics. These elements are all woven by Dvořák into a movement that is also sophisticated in its thematic processes and tonal design.

The finale of the *Dumky* Trio has a free rondo-like structure based on the alternating tempos typical of *dumky*:

Lento maestoso (m. 1)

Vivace (m. 23)

Lento (m. 87)

Vivace (m. 132)

Poco meno–Vivace (m. 164)

This is no conventional rondo, however, since the returns are not literal, and there is thematic overlap among the sections, especially in the last, which also serves as a kind of coda.

The finale is held together by the recurrence and constant transformation of two main themes. The first, a flourish spanning an octave descent from G to G, is introduced by the piano in measures 1–2 and 5–6, and tends to dominate the slow sections. The other, more prominent theme, associated mainly with the fast sections, is built on a figure that oscillates between two notes a third apart. This motive is introduced in the piano in measure 9, then appears simultaneously in different rhythmic values in the piano and violin (mm. 17–22). At the Vivace (m. 23), the theme at lasts bursts forth in its complete form, now as a folk dance in a pounding duple meter. Even at such moments Dvořák displays his contrapuntal skill: the theme, in the violin, is ornamented by a countertheme played by the cello in the same range.

Dvořák harmonizes the Vivace theme in a different manner each time it appears. At measure 23, its oscillating figure is accompanied by a bold alternation between a first-inversion tonic C minor and the flatted sixth, A♭ major. In measure 30, the piano plays the theme in octaves over drone-like repeated tonic and subdominant chords. A few moments later, Dvořák makes striking use of the augmented E♭ triad in alternation with the subdominant and flatted-sixth chords (mm. 42–46).

Dvořák achieves a magical effect by shifting between minor and major versions of the same harmony. In the first Vivace, Dvořák moves abruptly from C minor to C major (m. 61). The dynamic drops to *pp*, then *ppp*, and the main theme now appears in major (m. 65) over a sustained C pedal point. The transformation of the theme from its first appearance in measure 23 is astonishing, yet utterly convincing.

Dvořák reserves still more surprises for the next appearance of the Vivace (m. 132). The main theme is at first harmonized in F minor, returning to the tonic in measure 140. In measure 148 Dvořák suddenly transposes the theme upward to the Neapolitan D♭, the most remote harmonic-thematic shift so far in the movement and a fulfillment of the earlier emphasis on the note D♭.

The final section (mm. 164–206) serves as both a return and a coda, bringing back the two main themes simultaneously in the key of C major. The cello plays the slower theme, the violin the faster one. Dvořák adds new harmonic touches in the harmony and voice-leading. Raising the G to G♯ yields a C-augmented triad (mm. 165–66); with the rise of another half step, from G♯ to A, we arrive in A minor (m. 168). Near the end of the coda Dvořák reiterates the Neapolitan chord one last time (m. 198), propelling the movement to its lively conclusion.

Tristan und Isolde: Act 1, Scene 3, Isolde's Narrative
Opera, 1859

From Richard Wagner, *Tristan and Isolde*. New York: Edwin F. Kalmus.

wo er auch steh', so sag-te er, ge-treu-lich dien' er ihr, der Frau-en höch-ster

Ehr'; liess' er das Steu-er jetzt zur Stund', wie lenkt' er si-cher den

Etwas zurückhaltend.

ISOLDE (schmerzlich bitter).

(sehr gedehnt)

Kiel zu König Marke's Land? „Wie lenkt' er sicher den Kiel zu

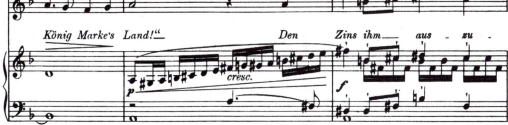

Wieder sehr lebhaft.

(grell und heftig)

König Marke's Land!" Den Zins ihm aus zu-

82 lag. I-sol-de's Kunst ward ihm be-kannt, mit Heil-sal-ben

88 und Balsam-saft der Wun-de, die ihn plag-te, ge-treu-lich pflag sie

riten.

93 a tempo *Immer belebter.* da. Der „Tan-tris" mit sor-gender List sich nannte, als

97 *Schneller.* „Tri-stan" I-sold' ihn bald er-kann-te, da in des

heilt' ich, dass er ge - sun - de, und heim nach Hau - se keh - re, — mit dem Blick mich

nicht mehr beschwe - re!   O Wun - der!

Wo hatt' ich die Au - gen? Der Gast, den einst ich pfle - gen half, Sein

Lob hör - test du e - ben: — „Hei! unser Held Tri -

Ei - de hält!—

Den als Tan - tris un - erkannt ich ent_

las - sen, als Tri - stan kehrt er kühn zu - rück; auf stol - zem

Schiff, von ho - hem Bord, Ir - lands Er - bin begehrt' er zur

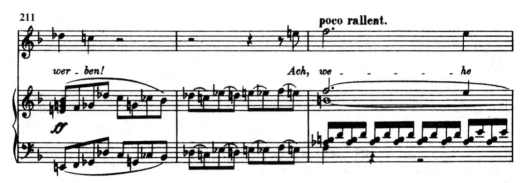

Isolde and Brangäne alone, all the curtains closed again. Isolde raises herself with a gesture of hopelessness and rage. Brangäne falls at her feet.

BRANGÄNE

Weh, ach wehe!	*Alas, alas!*
Dies zu dulden!	*To endure this!*

ISOLDE *on the verge of a terrible outburst, quickly recovering herself*

Doch nun von Tristan!	*What now from Tristan?*
Genau will ich's vernehmen.	*I wish to hear exactly!*

BRANGÄNE

Ach, frage nicht!	*Ah, do not ask!*

ISOLDE

Frei sag's ohne Furcht!	*Speak freely without fear!*

BRANGÄNE

Mit höf'schen Worten	*With courteous words*
wich er aus.	*he was evasive.*

ISOLDE

Doch als du deutlich mahntest?	*But when you warned him clearly?*

BRANGÄNE

Da ich zur Stell'	*When to this spot*
ihn zu dir rief:	*I bade him come to you:*
wo er auch steh',	*where he was standing,*
so sagte er,	*he said*
getreulich dien' er ihr,	*he faithfully serves you,*
der Frauen höchster Ehr';	*the most honorable of women;*
ließ' er das Steuer	*were he to leave the helm*
jetzt zur Stund',	*just now,*
wie lenkt' er sicher den Kiel	*how could he safely steer the ship*
zu König Markes Land?	*to King Mark's land?*

ISOLDE *with bitter irony*

"Wie lenkt' er sicher den Kiel	*"How could he safely steer the ship*
zu König Markes Land?"	*to King Mark's land?"*

harshly and violently

Den Zins ihm auszuzahlen,
den er aus Irland zog!

To pay him the tribute
he took from Ireland!

BRANGÄNE

Auf deine eignen Worte,
als ich ihm die entbot,
ließ seinen Diener Kurwenal —

To your own words,
as I relayed them to him,
he let his servant Kurwenal answer—

ISOLDE

Den hab ich wohl vernommen,
kein Wort, das mir entging.
Erfuhrest du meine Schmach,
nun höre, was sie mir schuf.
Wie lachend sie
mir Lieder singen,
wohl könnt' auch ich erwidern!
Von einem Kahn,
der klein und arm
an Irlands Küsten schwamm,
darinnen krank
ein siecher Mann
elend im Sterben lag.
Isoldes Kunst
ward ihm bekannt;
mit Heilsalben
und Balsamsaft
der Wunde, die ihn plagte,
getreulich pflag sie da.
Der "Tantris"
mit sorgender List sich nannte,
als "Tristan"
Isold' ihn bald erkannte,
da in des Müß'gen Schwerte
eine Scharte sie gewahrte,
darin genau
sich fügt'ein Splitter,
den einst im Haupt
des Iren-Ritter,
zum Hohn ihr heimgesandt,
mit kund'ger Hand sie fand.

I understood him well,
No word escaped me.
If you experienced my shame,
Now hear how it happened.
As they laughingly
sing songs to me,
I could well respond!
About how a boat,
small and frail,
floated to Ireland's coast,
therein sick,
an ailing man
lay suffering and near death.
Isolde's art
became known to him;
with healing salves
and soothing lotions
the wound that tormented him
she faithfully cared for.
"Tantris,"
as he called himself with careful cunning,
as "Tristan"
Isolde soon recognized him,
since in the powerless man's sword
she saw a notch,
which exactly
fitted a splinter,
which once in the head
of the Irish knight,
sent home to her in scorn,
she found with skilled hand.

Da schrie's mir auf	*I then cried out*
aus tiefstem Grund!	*from my deepest soul!*
Mit dem hellen Schwert	*With that gleaming sword*
ich vor ihm stund,	*I stood before him,*
an ihm, dem Überfrechen,	*on him, the impudent man,*
Herrn Morolds Tod zu rächen.	*to avenge Lord Morold's death.*
Von seinem Lager	*From his bed*
blickt' er her —	*he looked up —*
nicht auf das Schwert,	*not at the sword,*
nicht auf die Hand —	*not at my hand —*
er sah mir in die Augen.	*he looked into my eyes.*
Seines Elendes	*His suffering*
jammerte mich! —	*distressed me! —*
Das Schwert — ich ließ es fallen!	*The sword — I let it fall!*
Die Morold schlug, die Wunde,	*The wound that Morold struck,*
sie heilt' ich, daß er gesunde	*I healed it, so that, healed,*
und heim nach Hause kehre,	*he could return home,*
mit dem Blick mich nicht mehr beschwere!	*and no longer trouble me with his gaze!*

BRANGÄNE

O Wunder! Wo hatt' ich die Augen?	*Oh, wonder! Where were my eyes?*
Der Gast, den einst	*The guest, whom once*
ich pflegen half?	*I helped to nurse?*

ISOLDE

Sein Lob hörtest du eben:	*Just now you heard him praised:*
Hei! Unser Held Tristan —	*"Hey! Our hero Tristan" —*
der war jener traur'ge Mann.	*That was our sad man.*
Er schwur mit tausend Eiden	*With a thousand oaths he swore*
mir ew'gen Dank und Treue!	*eternal gratitude and loyalty to me!*
Nun hör, wie ein Held	*Now hear how a hero*
Eide hält!	*keeps his oath!*
Den als Tantris	*He whom as Tantris*
unerkannt ich entlassen,	*I released unrecognized,*
als Tristan	*as Tristan*
kehrt' er kühn zurück;	*came boldly back;*
auf stolzem Schiff,	*on a proud ship,*
von hohem Bord,	*with a high bow,*
Irlands Erbin	*Ireland's heiress*
begehrt' er zur Eh'	*he asked as bride*
für Kornwalls müden König,	*for Cornwall's weary king,*

für Marke, seinen Ohm.	*for Mark, his uncle.*
Da Morold lebte,	*Had Morold lived,*
wer hätt' es gewagt	*who would have dared*
uns je solche Schmach zu bieten?	*to offer me such shame?*
Für der zinspflicht'gen	*For the vassal*
Kornen Fürsten	*prince of the Cornish*
um Irlands Krone zu werben!	*To seek Ireland's crown!*
Ach, wehe mir!	*Ah, woe is me!*
Ich ja war's,	*It was I*
die heimlich selbst	*who in secret*
die Schmach sich schuf!	*brought shame on myself!*
Das rächende Schwert,	*The avenging sword,*
statt es zu schwingen,	*instead of wielding it,*
machtlos ließ ich's fallen!	*powerless I let it fall!*
Nun dien' ich dem Vasallen!	*Now I serve the vassal!*

BRANGÄNE

Da Friede, Sühn' und Freundschaft	*When peace, truce, and friendship*
von allen ward beschworen,	*were sworn by all,*
wir freuten uns all' des Tags;	*we all rejoiced in that day;*
wie ahnte mir da,	*how I could I have foreseen,*
daß dir es Kummer schüf'?	*that it would cause you grief?*

—Richard Wagner

At the heart of this scene from Act 1 of *Tristan und Isolde* is the segment frequently referred to as Isolde's Narrative, in which she bitterly tells her companion Brangäne of an earlier encounter with the knight Tristan, who is now carrying her on a ship to marry his uncle, King Mark. The narrative provides an excellent example of how Wagner constructs his scenes not from traditional "numbers," but from a sequence of more open-ended structures he called "poetic-musical periods." Although Wagner's musical language is highly chromatic and fluid, with frequent modulation, his periods are often organized around a central tonal area. In Isolde's Narrative, after an introductory segment (mm. 1–65), there are two such units, both indicated by key signatures. The first (mm. 66–174) is anchored in E minor, but with frequent harmonic diversions, including deceptive cadences to C major. The second (mm. 175–230) is primarily in F major, and concludes with a cadence and change of key signature to F minor. Individual phrase structures are often quite regular. At measures 75–82, for example, Wagner sets each three-line unit of text as a phrase of four measures, arranged like a traditional antecedent and consequent. The first phrase cadences deceptively to C major, the second to the tonic E minor.

As is characteristic in Wagner's mature operas, Isolde's Narrative is structured thematically around leitmotifs, themes that take on psychological and dramatic significance as they recur across an opera. At the beginning of a scene or period, Wagner introduces a new theme that gradually becomes interwoven with earlier themes. This theme, which is previewed in the orchestra in measures 9–11 and then becomes a more structural element at the turn to E minor (m. 66), is sometimes called the "Ailing Tristan" theme because of its association with Isolde's healing of the wounded knight. The melody descends in dotted rhythms and chromatic steps over a bass line that rises chromatically in semitones. This leitmotif returns, with its notes extended, to conclude Isolde's Narrative (mm. 213–20). After its initial appearance in Act 1, scene 3, the "Ailing Tristan" theme reappears in the opera at dramatically appropriate moments, most notably at the beginning of Act 3, when Tristan, newly wounded by Melot's sword, awaits Isolde.

In Isolde's Narrative, the "Ailing Tristan" theme acts as a kind of ritornello or refrain. In between its appearances come other themes that have been heard earlier in the opera, including a fanfare-like theme associated with Tristan as hero (m. 97); an agitated, disjunct chromatic figure sometimes called the "Anger" theme (mm. 181–83); and, more significant, the most important leitmotif in the opera, the "Desire" theme of rising semitones, first heard in the Prelude. In Isolde's Narrative, "Desire" occurs at the moment when Isolde relates how Tristan gazed lovingly in her eyes as he lay on his sickbed (mm. 130–34). The orchestra plays the theme; then, as if first realizing her emotions of love, Isolde sings it. Here, as so often in Wagner, the orchestra seems to represent the character's subconscious, revealing to us more about Isolde's true feelings for Tristan than she herself is initially aware of.

Wagner's skills as a musical psychologist are even more evident when we realize that the "Desire" theme is really a free inversion of the "Ailing Tristan" (or vice versa):

Wagner emphasizes the relationship when he underpins "Ailing Tristan" with a rising chromatic bass line that is an augmented form of "Desire" (C♯–D–D♯–E, mm. 66–68). The latent unity between these two themes reveals more powerfully than words the doomed attraction between Tristan and Isolde.

Rigoletto: Act 3, Scene 3, Quartet

Opera, 1851

From Giuseppe Verdi, *Rigoletto, Vocal Score*. New York: Edwin F. Kalmus.

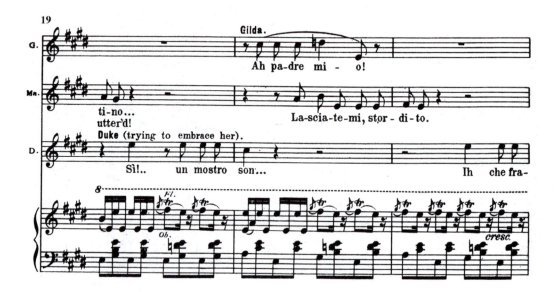

son de' vez - zi tuo - i; con un detto, un det - to sol tu

puo - i le mie pe - ne, le mie pe - ne con - so - lar. Vieni, e

sen - ti del mio co - re il fre - quente pal - pi - tar, con un

detto, un det - to sol tu puo - i le mie pe - ne, le mie pe - ne con - so -

Gilda and Rigoletto in the street, the Duke and Maddalena on the ground floor

DUKE

Un dì, se ben rammentomi,	*One day, if I recall correctly,*
o bella, t'incontrai . . .	*O lovely one, I met you . . .*
Mi piacque di te chiedere,	*I was pleased to ask about you,*
e intesi che qui stai.	*and learned that you live here.*
Or sappi, che d'allora	*Now know that since then*
sol te quest'alma adora.	*my soul worships you alone.*

GILDA

Iniquo!	*Traitor!*

MADDALENA

Ah, ah! . . . e vent'altre appresso	*Ah! And some twenty others*
le scorda forse adesso?	*you are perhaps forgetting?*
Ha un'aria, il signorino,	*You have the air, young man,*
da vero libertino . . .	*Of a true libertine . . .*

DUKE

Sì! . . . un mostro son . . .	*Yes, I'm a monster . . .*

goes to embrace her

GILDA

Ah padre mio!	*Ah, father!*

MADDALENA

Lasciatemi,	*Leave me alone,*
stordito.	*Foolish man.*

DUKE

Eh, che fracasso!	*Oh, what a fuss!*

MADDALENA

Stia saggio.	*Behave yourself.*

DUKE

E tu sii docile,
non fare mi tanto chiasso.
Ogni saggezza chiudesi
nel gaudio e nell'amore.

And you be nice,
Don't be so noisy.
All good behavior ends
in pleasure and in love.

takes her hand

La bella mano candida!

What a beautiful white hand!

MADDALENA

Scherzate voi, signore.

You're joking, sir.

DUKE

No, no.

No, no.

MADDALENA

Son brutta.

I'm ugly.

DUKE

Abbracciami.

Embrace me.

GILDA

Iniquo!

Traitor!

MADDALENA

Ebro!

You are drunk!

DUKE (*laughing*)

D'amor ardente.

With passionate love.

MADDALENA

Signor l'indifferente,
vi piace canzonar?

Indifferent sir,
Do you like to tease?

DUKE

No, no, ti vo'sposar.

No, I want to marry you.

MADDALENA

Ne voglio la parola . . .

I want your word of honor . . .

DUKE (*ironically*)

Amabile figliuola!

Lovable maid!

RIGOLETTO (*to Gilda, who has seen and understood everything*)

E non ti basta ancor?

Is that not yet enough for you?

GILDA

Iniquo traditor!

Villainous traitor!

DUKE

Bella figlia dell'amore,
schiavo son de'vezzi tuoi;
con un detto sol tu puoi
le mie pene consolar.
Vieni, e senti del mio core
il frequente palpitar.

Fair daughter of love,
I am a slave to your charms;
with but one word you could
relieve my sufferings.
Come, and feel in my heart
the constant beating.

MADDALENA

Ah! ah! rido ben di core,
chè tai baie costan poco;
quanto valga il vostro giuoco,
mel credete, so apprezzar.
Sono avvezza, bel signore,
ad un simile scherzar.

Ah! I am really laughing,
Since such talk costs little;
how much your game is worth,
believe me, I am able to tell.
I'm accustomed, handsome sir,
to such joking.

GILDA

Ah! così parlar d'amore
a me pur l'infame ho udito!
Infelice cor tradito,
per angoscia non scoppiar.

Ah! speaking thus of love
I too have heard the scoundrel do to me.
Unhappy betrayed heart,
Do not burst with anguish.

RIGOLETTO (*to Gilda*)

Taci, il piangere non vale;
ch'ei mentiva sei sicura.
Taci, e mia sarà la cura

Be quiet, weeping is of no use;
that he was lying you are certain.
Be quiet, and mine will be the task

la vendetta d'affrettar.	*To hasten revenge.*
Sì, pronta fia sarà fatale,	*Yes, it will be quick and fatal,*
io saprollo fulminar.	*I will know how to strike at him.*

—Francesco Maria Piave

Rigoletto, which premiered in 1851, is one of Verdi's most popular operas, a powerful musical drama of familial and romantic love, of deception, retribution, and, eventually, tragic death. The libretto, prepared by Verdi's regular collaborator of the period, Francesco Piave, was based on a play by the French dramatist Victor Hugo. In this story Verdi found what he always looked for in his dramatic sources: distinctive characters and "strong" situations in which they could interact.

The quartet from Act 3 of *Rigoletto* is a wonderful example of Verdi's mastery in rendering such characters and situations. At a remote inn on the outskirts of town, we encounter four of the opera's main characters, each a different voice type: the flirtatious Duke (tenor); the newest target of his passion, Maddalena (contralto); the once trusting, but now disillusioned Gilda (soprano); and her despairing, vengeful father Rigoletto (baritone). The scene has two independent but interacting dramatic levels: the Duke and Maddalena are inside the inn; Gilda and Rigoletto watch from the outside. Opera has an advantage over spoken drama in that characters can sing simultaneously; the possibility of different vocal registers (in this case, four) and different melodic shapes allows us to take in all their thoughts and actions.

The quartet is in two large sections, an introductory Allegro in E major ("Un dì, se ben rammentomi") and a spacious Andante in Db major ("Bella figlia dell'amore"). In the Allegro, Verdi uses the technique known as *parlante* (literally, "speaking"), in which the orchestra provides the main continuity through the presentation and development of an instrumental theme, while the singers switch more freely between lyrical and speech-like utterances. Verdi has the opening orchestral melody subtly shadow but not double the Duke's vocal line, almost as if commenting on his character. The violins regularly add a dissonant A♯ appoggiatura to the upbeat, thus clashing momentarily with the Duke's note B: something is not right about the deceitful, inebriated Duke, disguised as a cavalry officer. The repeated octave leaps in the violin (m. 3) and the spirited trills (m. 8) further convey his superficial nature. The octave leaps also constitute an ironic reminiscence (at the same pitch level and in the same key) of a musical figure from Gilda's Act 1 aria "Caro nome" (Beloved name), about her attraction to the Duke.

The introduction comes to an abrupt end on a G♯-major triad, which serves as the pivot to the Andante. It is the dominant of both C♯ minor, where the introduction has moved in its final six measures, and (enharmonically) of the subsequent Db major, a strikingly different key from the initial E major that helps changes the mood and dramatic situation. In the Andante, Verdi's genius at ensemble writing is at its most developed. Each singer contributes a distinct melodic style that reflects his or her character. The broad lyrical phrases of the Duke reveal his swaggering confidence and sensual appeal. Based upon his melodies alone, we can understand why women fall in love with him. Maddalena, who is attracted to him but suspicious, sings in nervous, staccato sixteenth notes. Gilda also sings in sixteenth notes, but legato ones, characterized by short two-note appoggiatura figures and rests that create the effect of sobs. In her part, Verdi frequently emphasizes the anguished words "no" and "non." Rigoletto, singing at the bottom of the texture, has mostly static and slow-moving lines that capture his grim determination to seek revenge. But at moments he bursts out passionately into accented sixteenth notes that convey at once smoldering anger and empathy with his daughter.

◎ Norton Opera Sampler video available

Carmen: **Act 1, No. 5,** *Habanera*

Opera, 1875

From George Bizet, *Carmen*. New York: Schirmer.

fait, menace ou pri - è - re, L'un par - le bien, l'au-tre se tait; Et c'est

l'au-tre que je pré - fè - re Il n'a rien dit; — mais il me

plait. — L'a - mour! — l'a -

L'a-mour est un oi-seau re - bel - le Que nul ne peut ap-pri-voi-

L'a-mour est un oi-seau re - bel - le Que nul ne peut ap-pri-voi-

72 *portamento.*

là! Tout au - tour de toi vi - te, vi - te, Il vient, s'en va, __ puis il re -

76 *portamento.*

vient; Tu crois le te - nir, il t'é - vi - te; Tu crois l'é - vi - ter, __ il te

80

tient! __ L'a - mour! __ l'a -

Sopr. *pp legg.*

Tout au - tour de toi vi - te, vite Il vient, s'en va, puis il re -

Ten. *pp legg.*

CARMEN

L'amour est un oiseau rebelle	*Love is a rebellious bird*
que nul ne peut apprivoiser,	*that no one can tame,*
et c'est bien en vain qu'on l'appelle,	*and one calls it only in vain,*
s'il lui convient de refuser!	*If it chooses to say no!*
Rien n'y fait, menace ou prière,	*Nothing works, threat or prayer,*
l'un parle bien, l'autre se tait;	*one man speaks well, the other is silent;*
et c'est l'autre que je préfère,	*it's the other I prefer,*
il n'a rien dit, mais il me plait.	*he has said nothing, but pleases me.*

CIGARETTE GIRLS, YOUNG MEN

L'amour est un oiseau rebelle, *etc.*	*Love is a rebellious bird, etc.*

CARMEN

L'amour est enfant de Bohème,	*Love is a Gypsy child,*
il n'a jamais, jamais connu de loi,	*It has never, never known a law,*

si tu ne m'aimes pas, je t'aime,	*if you don't love me, then I love you,*
si je t'aime, prends garde à toi!	*if I love you, watch out for yourself!*

CIGARETTE GIRLS, YOUNG MEN, WORKING MEN

Prends garde à toi!	*Watch out for yourself!*

CARMEN

Si tu ne m'aimes pas, je t'aime!	*If you don't love me, then I love you,*

CIGARETTE GIRLS, YOUNG MEN, WORKING MEN

Prends garde à toi!	*Watch out for yourself!*

CARMEN

Mais si je t'aime, prends garde à toi!	*But if I love you, watch out for yourself!*

CIGARETTE GIRLS, YOUNG MEN, WORKING MEN

L'amour est enfant de Bohème, *etc.*	*Love is a Gypsy child, etc.*

CARMEN

L'oiseau que tu croyais surprendre	*The bird you thought to have caught*
battit de l'aile et s'envola;	*beat its wings and flew away;*
l'amour est loin, tu peux l'attendre,	*love is far away, you can wait for it,*
tu ne l'attends plus, il est là.	*When you don't expect it, it is there!*
Tout autour de toi, vite, vite,	*All around you, swiftly, swiftly,*
il vient, s'en va, puis il revient;	*it comes, goes, then comes again;*
tu crois le tenir, il t'évite,	*you think you hold it, it flees from you,*
tu crois l'éviter, il te tient!	*you try to flee it, it holds you fast!*

CIGARETTE GIRLS, YOUNG MEN, WORKING MEN

Tout autour de toi, vite, vite, *etc.*	*All around you, swiftly, swiftly, etc.*

CARMEN

L'amour!	*Love!*
L'amour est enfant de Bohème, *etc.*	*Love is a Gypsy child, etc.*

—Ludovic Halévy and Henri Meilhac

In the *Habanera* from Act 1 of Bizet's *Carmen*, one of the most famous characters in all opera introduces herself to us and to her onstage listeners. The *Habanera* is what is sometimes called a "diegetic" number: it is performed as a song and is perceived as such by the other characters within the opera itself. Carmen, a Gypsy cigarette girl, rarely sings alone or to herself, and she often dances for others. The text and music of the *Habanera* capture the complex personality of the character—attention-grabbing and seductive, yet defiantly independent.

Although Carmen and the music associated with her in the opera are meant to be understood as Spanish, the *Habanera* in fact derives from an Afro-Cuban dance (the name comes from Havana, the capital city of Cuba) that is moderately slow but lilting, in $\frac{2}{4}$ meter, and characterized by the repetition of a basic rhythmic pattern (long-short-long-long) and the use of triplets against the prevailing duple articulation. Bizet lifted his *Habanera* directly from a song by the Spanish composer Sebastián de Iradier (1809–1865). He closely followed Iradier's melody and the structure of alternating minor and major keys. Apparently believing this was a common popular song, Bizet did not credit Iradier; when Iradier objected, Bizet included a footnote reference to him in the *Carmen* score.

Bizet might have borrowed the *Habanera* tune, but only a composer of his genius could have tailored it so closely to the main character, who is at once direct and alluring. The *Habanera* is in a strophic form with two eight-line stanzas ("L'amour est un oiseau rebelle," mm. 4–28, and "L'oiseau que tu croyais surprendre," mm. 64–88) and a refrain ("L'amour est enfant de Bohème," mm. 28–61 and 88–120), which are punctuated by echoes from the chorus. The ostinato accompaniment pattern, with its repetitious rhythms and D pedal point, reveals not only Carmen's steady determination, but also her ability to captivate her listeners by sheer persistence.

At the same time, Carmen's melodic line is sinuous and fluid. It begins with a descent in half steps from the tonic to the dominant and then features little flourishes of triplet eighth notes ("est un oi-," m. 5) and sixteenth notes ("peut," m. 7). Bizet draws on the long association of chromaticism and of rhythmic ornament with the erotic and the exotic. Especially in the nineteenth century, such techniques were often used in opera or instrumental music to depict an "Other" (often Middle Eastern, Asian, or Gypsy) seen as foreign to the prevailing Western European culture. Like Carmen, such figures were both attractive and threatening. The words of the *Habanera* also reinforce this stereotype of the Gypsy: she is rebellious, passionate, and elusive.

It is common in opera for an onstage chorus to react or interact by singing the same material as the main character, as happens in the *Habanera*. But here Bizet gives that practice a special dramatic meaning. When they echo Carmen's phrases—and fill them out with harmonies—the cigarette girls and the men of the crowd are at least momentarily falling under her powerful spell. Bizet's orchestration subtly enhances this impression. When Carmen sings the *Habanera* alone, she is accompanied by conventional instruments. Only when the chorus enters does Bizet bring in the exotic ones—the triangle and tambourine. It is as though, completely enthralled by Carmen, the chorus imagines these sonorities along with her melodies.

🄯 **Norton Opera Sampler video available**

JOHANNES BRAHMS (1833–1897)

Symphony No. 1 in C Minor, Op. 68: Movement 1
Symphony, 1876

From Johannes Brahms, *Complete Symphonies in Full Orchestral Score.* New York: Dover Publications, Inc.

Brahms completed his First Symphony in 1876, after a gestational process of 14 long years. Like many composers of his generation, he labored to come out from under Beethoven's enormous shadow by adding his own individual creative voice to the Classical symphonic tradition and the Romantic symphonic legacy of Schubert, Schumann, and Mendelssohn. By any measure, Brahms succeeded. His four symphonies are touchstones of today's concert repertory, admired for their originality and power of expression.

SONATA FORM	Slow introduction	Exposition				Development	Recapitulation				Coda
THEME		1	Trans.	2	Closing		1	Trans.	2	Closing	
KEY	c → G (as V)	c		E♭	e♭	modulates	c	C	c		c → C
MEASURE	1	38	97	121	157	189	343	370	394	430	462

The first movement of Brahms's First is in sonata form, framed by a spacious slow introduction and coda. This basic structure had been common since the symphonies of Haydn almost a century earlier. But Brahms's symphonic style is set apart from that of his predecessors by intense motivic-thematic work, rhythmic and metrical complexity, dense counterpoint, and rich chromaticism. These features sometimes obscure the internal divisions of the form. Although measure numbers are provided in the diagram above, the boundaries between the traditional elements of the sonata exposition—theme 1, transition, theme 2, and closing theme—are fluid in Brahms's movement. These elements are further compressed and abbreviated in the recapitulation.

The main "theme" of the first group of the exposition is really a complex of three motivic ideas:

These motives permeate all parts of the orchestral texture. Motives *x* and *y*, which are mainly stepwise, first appear in the top melodic voice in measures 38–41, and then as counterpoint underpinning the more triadic motive *z* in measures 42–45. As is common in symphonic movements from the Classical and Romantic eras, the slow introduction of Brahms's First presents in fragmentary form the main thematic elements of the movement. In this unforgettable opening, the ideas seem to take shape out of chaos. Over a throbbing pedal point on the tonic C, played by timpani, horns, contrabassoons, and double basses, the other strings and woodwinds begin to outline the chromatic elements that will coalesce into motive *x*. The introduction modulates to the dominant G (m. 9), where an episode anticipates other ideas from the Allegro, including pairs of descending sevenths (mm. 9–10) and an oscillating neighbor-note figure (mm. 11–12). After the introduction of *z* (mm. 21–24), the pedal and motivic complex return on the dominant and build up enormous tension that is released only at the start of the exposition.

Rhythmic intensity and a propulsive ⁶⁄₈ meter give the main Allegro the character of a scherzo, one that rarely settles down into stable, lyrical melodies. The motivic complex of x, y, and z governs almost the entire movement. The second group, which begins at measure 121 in the relative major, E♭ (a conventional secondary key area for an exposition in minor), is a reworking of the main theme of the first group; motive z is in the cellos and x in the woodwinds. The closing group is based on a segment of the y motive, a descending stepwise third, and is distinctive for bringing the exposition to a conclusion in E♭ minor, which is not a traditional move, but here helps to set up the analogous C-minor conclusion of the recapitulation (mm. 458–61), before the coda.

Throughout the exposition, the listener is kept on edge not only by the relentless motivic activity and harmonic instability, but also by the rhythmic-metric ambiguities that are a hallmark of Brahms's style. Brahms often places strong accents on normally weak parts of a measure. Sometimes these beats are tied over to the downbeat of the next measure, as in measures 9–19 (beats 5 and 6) and measures 59–69 (beat 4, in lower, then upper strings). When this process extends over long stretches, we lose our metrical bearings. The accented beats come to sound like actual downbeats, and the notated meter seems to be displaced.

Brahms infuses his exposition with such extensive thematic "development" that he has a challenge to maintain variety and momentum in the development section. He achieves that goal by fashioning yet another theme out of the basic motives. At measures 232–36 motive y (desending stepwise fourth and ascending second, D♭–C♭–B♭–A♭–B♭) is supplemented on either side to create a broad, heroic tune in dotted quarter notes, which is developed over almost thirty measures. The lead-up to the recapitulation is especially exciting. At measure 273, motive x appears (again in both rising and descending forms) over a dominant pedal, which is sustained until measure 290 as the dynamics drop to pianissimo. A gradual crescendo leads to another long dominant pedal, now fortissimo (m. 321). We expect this dominant to resolve to the tonic and for the recapitulation to get underway. But Brahms prepares a surprising detour. At measure 335 the bass G drops suddenly to F♯, which supports a B-minor triad. Only eight measures later (m. 343) do things right themselves as the z motive returns in the tonic to begin the recapitulation.

The coda begins with a powerful overflow of rhythmic energy from the end of the recapitulation, building to a huge climax at measure 474. Then Brahms applies the brakes, as motive x reappears and the tempo is slowed to accommodate a modified return of the slow introduction, with its pulsating tonic pedal point (Meno allegro, m. 495). At measure 504 the coda turns unexpectedly to the tonic major and ends quietly in that key. But after so much turbulence in the movement, this conclusion has residual tension, which will be resolved unequivocally only much later in the triumphant coda of the symphony's finale.

Symphony No. 6 in B Minor (*Pathétique*), Op. 74: Movement 4

Symphony, 1893

From Peter Ilyitch Tchaikovsky, *Fourth, Fifth and Sixth Symphonies*. New York: Dover Publications, Inc.

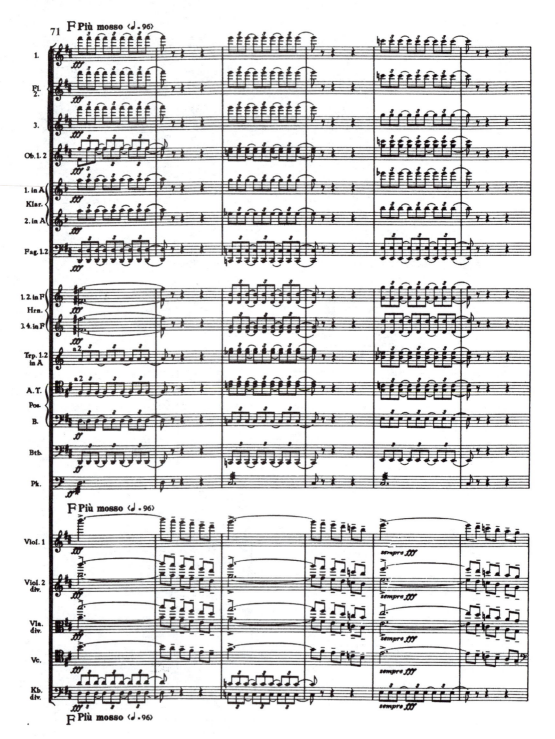

Tchaikovsky composed his last symphony over a period of seven months in 1893. He conducted the premiere in October 1893 and died suddenly nine days later, most likely from cholera contracted by drinking unboiled water in the midst of an epidemic.

Ever since the symphony's premiere, critics and audiences have speculated about its title, possible programmatic meaning, and relationship to the composer's own life. In fact, Tchaikovsky avoided providing any specific program for the work. He affixed the famous title only after the first performance. The Russian adjective *Pateticheskaia* (usually rendered in French as "Pathétique"), does not indicate "pathos" in the sense of suffering, but rather a more general emotional quality like "impassioned" or "passionate." The composer's brother Modest, as close to an authoritative source as we are likely to get, later reported that the symphony expressed the differing moods, high and low, that Tchaikovsky had experienced in his life.

The disposition of the four movements of Tchaikovsky's Sixth is distinctive in that the slow movement comes last. (Gustav Mahler would attempt something similar in his Third [1896] and Ninth Symphonies [1909].) The first movement is a spacious, lyrical sonata form. The two inner movements are both faster and dance-related: the second is like a lilting waltz, but cast in $\frac{5}{4}$ meter; the third combines the elements of a scherzo and a march.

We need no explicit program or statement from the composer to experience the finale, marked Adagio lamentoso, as one of the most searing, tragic movements in the symphonic literature. Its basic structure is characteristic of many slow movements: a broad binary form with no separate development section. There are two main themes that stand in relationship to each other like first and second themes in a sonata exposition, one in B minor and the other first heard in the relative major, D, and then later brought into the tonic. Such a description gives little idea of the skill with which Tchaikovsky treats the themes or of the powerful passages of climax and transition that come in between the large statements.

SONATA FORM	Exposition			Recapitulation		
SUBSECTION	A	B	climax, catastrophe, retransition	A′	transition with trombone chorale	B′/Coda
KEY	b	D	modulatory	b	b	b
MEASURE	1	39	70	90	137	147

The **A** theme is distinctive in that its melodic pitches are divided between the first and second violins. The theme thus sounds different to the ear than it looks on paper. When it reappears at measure 90, the melody is given only to the first violins. In Tchaikovsky's day, the first and second violins were separated on either side of the podium. He thus clearly intended for listeners to distinguish between the antiphonal effect in the exposition and the unison in the recapitulation. Although some orchestras are now returning to that seating style, such subtle effects are lost in many performances and recordings today because conductors tend to place the violins all together on the left side of the stage.

Even though they are expressively very different from each other, the **A** and **B** themes share an important feature: both are based on stepwise motion descending through a fourth. The descending stepwise fourth was a musical emblem of lament in the Baroque period (as in Monteverdi's madrigal *Lament of the Nymph* of 1638), and Tchaikovsky may well have intended this association for the lamentoso finale of his Sixth. A sensitive musical psychologist, he fashioned the **A** and **B** themes to represent two different emotional aspects of the same musical gesture—in minor, despairing; in major, more hopeful.

The more positive emotion seems to dominate the **B** theme in the exposition, as it reverses its downward direction and rises chromatically (mm. 67–70). But at the climax (m. 71) it lands on a high B, and the harmony is wrenched back to the tonic, B minor, which is inflected by its own Neapolitan, C major. We sense that hope is lost, as the tempo increases and the strings spiral down to land on a *fortissimo* Neapolitan chord, followed by a fermata (m. 81). And now, as a transition to the recapitulation, the once radiant **B** theme is heard in minor, with dissonant harmonies (mm. 83–86).

After the restatement of the **A** theme in the recapitulation, Tchaikovsky introduces a new transition to **B** (m. 137), a low-lying, dark chorale-like passage for trombones and bass tuba, accompanied by the tam-tam or gong. The chorale is related to the finale's basic thematic material. It is a chromaticized and rhythamically augmented version of **A** without the first note (compare E–D–C♯–B–C♯ of mm. 1–2, divided between first and second violins, with D–C♯–B–A♯–B of mm. 137–44). With these unmistakably funereal sonorities the cloud of despair has now completely enveloped the finale. It also affects the final reappearance of the **B** theme (m. 147, Andante giusto), which serves as both reprise and coda. Theme **B** is now transposed to B minor, as we might expect in a recapitulation, but in the violas and cellos Tchaikovsky adds a chromatic imitative line, derived from **B**, that heightens the tension. In the final measures of the movement, the dynamics are reduced almost to silence, and all instruments drop out except the low strings. The last sonorities we hear, as devastating as any in Western music, are low Bs played *pppp* by divisi cellos and double basses.

LOUIS MOREAU GOTTSCHALK (1829–1869)

La gallina, danse cubaine

Character piece, ca. 1859

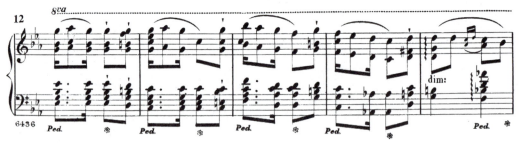

From *Piano Music of Louis Moreau Gottschalk*. New York: Dover Publications, Inc.

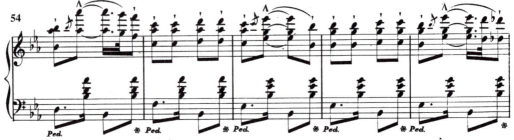

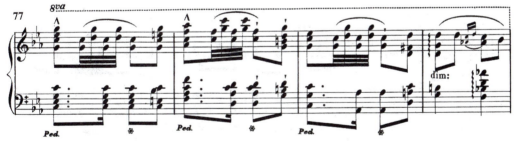

Between 1854 and 1862, the American-born composer-pianist Gottschalk made three extensive sojourns to the Spanish colony of Cuba, where he played concerts and immersed himself in the island culture. The indigenous music of Cuba inspired about 25 of Gottschalk's compositions, including three piano pieces published as "danses cubaines" (Cuban dances). *La gallina* (The Hen) was probably composed in Cuba in 1859; it was performed in New York in 1865 and published in versions for both solo and four-hands piano.

La gallina is modeled on the *contradanza*, the Cuban version of the European *contre-danse* brought over by French settlers. The *contradanza* enjoyed great popularity in Cuba in the nineteenth century. Normally danced by four couples facing each other, it was in a $\frac{2}{4}$ meter and comprised of 32-measure units. Gottschalk's concert *contradanzas* are based on two alternating themes corresponding to the *prima* and *segunda* units of the standard dance type, each measures long. Gottschalk merges this form with his own style based on elements of European Romantic piano music, especially variation and virtuosity. In *La gallina*, there are a total of eight 16-measure segments that alternate between themes. Theme 1 appears each time close to its original form, while theme 2 is subject to increasing elaboration in the manner of a theme and variations.

THEME	a	b	a	b (var. 1)	a	b (var. 2)	a	b (var. 3)
MEASURE	1	17	33	49	65	81	97	113

The infectious tunes of *La gallina* feature several different popular Cuban or Afro-Caribbean rhythmic patterns, including the *habanera* and the *amphibrach* (a term originally referring to a short-long-short metrical pattern in Classical Greek and Roman poetry):

The *habanera* would later become especially famous through its use in Bizet's opera *Carmen* (see Anthology 16). In measure 3 of *La gallina*, as often happens in the Cuban *contradanza*, the right hand plays the *amphibrach*, with its characteristic syncopated first beat, while the left hand plays the *habanera*.

As *La gallina* continues, theme **b** becomes progressively more elaborate. At measure 49 the right hand, which first played in thirds, is now in octaves. In its next appearance (m. 81), the melody of **b** is put in the left hand, which also has to play the bass notes. The right hand adds virtuosic ornamentation of repeated notes and arpeggios. In the last "variation" of **b** (m. 113), the melody is again in the left hand, while the right hand plays rapid sixteenth-note patterns.

Gottschalk's *La gallina*, ingeniously fusing Old and New World musical styles, anticipates by several decades the syncopated rhythms of ragtime and jazz that would become popular in the works of Scott Joplin and others.

AMY MARCY CHENEY BEACH (1867–1944)

Violin Sonata in A Minor, Op. 34: Movement 2

Violin sonata, 1896

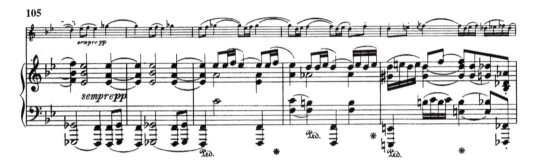

Amy Beach was a leading composer from the northeastern United States in the late nineteenth and early twentieth centuries. The only woman in the so-called New England School of composers centered in Boston, Beach made her later career in New York City.

   Her compositional output includes a symphony, songs, solo piano pieces, choral music, and 15 chamber works. She composed her four-movement Violin Sonata in six weeks in 1896. It was premiered on January 4, 1897, by Fritz Kneisel, concertmaster of the Boston Symphony Orchestra, with Beach at the piano.

   The second movement of the sonata is a scherzo with trio. It shows Beach's familiarity with several late-nineteenth-century composers, including Brahms, Dvořák, Fauré, and (perhaps) Debussy. Yet these influences are fully assimilated into Beach's individual voice—in the subtle treatment of form, the focused richness of the harmonic writing, the elegant use of counterpoint, and the propulsive motivic-rhythmic language.

SECTION	Scherzo			Trio	Scherzo (abbrev.)		Coda
SUBSECTION	A	B	A′		A	A′	
KEY	G → D		→ G	g	G		G
MEASURE	1	33	45	73	111	127	159

The main theme of the scherzo is at once accessible in its lively folklike spirit, and elusive in its contrapuntal and harmonic complexity. The theme unfolds in three-part imitation, shared among the violin and the left and right hands of the pianist. It begins away from the tonic G major, which arrives in root position only in measure 5. The theme's tonal profile is colored by modal elements, including the suggestion of an A Dorian scale (A–B–C–D–E–F♯–G) in measures 1–3, and the pentatonic scale (G–A–B–D–E) in measures 4–7.

The scherzo itself is a large-scale rounded binary form in which the first half, which is repeated, moves from the tonic to the dominant (reached at m. 25), though both harmonic areas remain fluid and unsettled. The return to **A′** after a developmental **B** segment is managed with great delicacy. We cannot point to a single moment where **A′** begins; it is not marked by any clear statement of the main theme from measure 1. In the diagram above, measure 45 is given as the moment of return mainly because of the reappearance of the opening motive at the original tempo. But the harmony here, a dominant seventh over B♭, with augmented fifth, still lies far away from the tonic. Only at measures 53–54, which correspond to measures 17–18, are we certain that we are back in **A′**. Here the piano lands on another augmented dominant seventh chord (D–F♯–A♯–C), which returns us to the realm of the tonic G. However, the tonic does appear definitively until the final cadence of **A′** at measures 71–72.

The trio, in a slower tempo and in the parallel minor, presents a striking contrast with the scherzo. For the first half of the trio (through m. 92), the violin lies at the very bottom of the texture, sustaining the lowest note (G) on its lowest string while the piano carries the thematic and harmonic continuity. The musical language of the trio is sometimes densely chromatic, as in the lines descending by half step in measures 82–85, and sometimes more modal, as in the cadence to G minor from an F-major chord (with the lowered leading tone F♮) in measures 90–92. Beach also introduces a whole-tone chord on the second beat of the first measure of the trio (m. 73). This is in fact the same augmented dominant seventh heard in measure 53 (with A♯ respelled as B♭). But the chord now "floats" more abstractly and coloristically.

The trio is linked thematically to the scherzo by the use of the neighbor-note motive of the scherzo's main theme (E–F♯–E, m. 1). This motive appears as part of the piano theme (G–A–G, mm. 73–74), and then in its original rhythm in the violin (mm. 76–85), where it bubbles up occasionally from the low held G. Beach creates an effective transition back to the scherzo (mm. 105–11) by reiterating the motive more frequently and by restoring the original registral placements of the two instruments, with the violin above the piano. The return of the scherzo (m. 111) is a compressed restatement of the original, in which the **B** section is omitted. As with the European composers who inspired her, Beach is able to strike a balance between accessibility and complexity. Her musical language is fluid and expressive, yet also anchored with solid technique.

21

GUSTAV MAHLER (1860–1911)

Lieder eines fahrenden Gesellen: No. 4, Die zwei blauen Augen

Song cycle, 1883–85; orchestrated ca. 1895

From Gustav Mahler, *Songs of a Wayfarer and Kindertotenlieder in Full Score*. New York: Dover Publications, Inc.

ihr mich an-ge-blickt? Nun hab ich e - wig Leid____ und Grä - men!

Die zwei blauen Augen von meinem Schatz,	*The two blue eyes of my sweetheart,*
Die haben mich in die weite Welt geschickt.	*They have sent me out into the wide world.*
Da mußt ich Abschied nehmen vom allerliebsten Platz!	*I had to take my leave from this beloved place!*
O Augen blau, warum habt ihr mich angeblickt?	*O blue eyes, why did you look at me?*
Nun hab' ich ewig Leid und Grämen.	*Now I have eternal suffering and grief.*
Ich bin ausgegangen in stiller Nacht	*I went out into the quiet night*
Wohl über die dunkle Heide.	*Far beyond the dark heath.*
Hat mir niemand Ade gesagt.	*No one said farewell to me.*
Ade! Mein Gesell' war Lieb' und Leide!	*Farewell! My companion was love and suffering!*
Auf der Straße steht ein Lindenbaum,	*On the road stands a linden tree,*
Da hab' ich zum ersten Mal im Schlaf geruht!	*There for the first time I found rest in sleep!*
Unter dem Lindenbaum,	*Under the linden tree,*
Der hat seine Blüten über mich geschneit,	*Which snowed its blossoms down upon me,*
Da wußt' ich nicht, wie das Leben tut,	*I knew nothing of how life works,*
War alles, alles wieder gut!	*Everything was good again!*
Alles! Alles, Lieb und Leid	*Everything! Everything, love and suffering*
Und Welt und Traum!	*And world and dream!*

—Gustav Mahler

For Gustav Mahler, the worlds of lieder and symphonic music were intimately connected. Many movements in his symphonies draw upon his own songs, which are either adapted for instruments or presented as a vocal solo with instrumental accompaniment. Mahler also wrote over 30 orchestral songs, some grouped into cycles that are among his primary works. His first cycle, *Lieder eines fahrenden Gesellen* (Songs of a Wayfarer), comprises four songs; it was composed in 1883–85 with piano, then orchestrated in the early 1890s.

Mahler was drawn to German poetry of the early Romantic period, in which images of nature and landscape serve as metaphors for the poet's feelings, usually of unrequited love. Mahler wrote his own texts for the *Songs of a Wayfarer* in imitation of poems from his favorite collection, *Des Knaben Wunderhorn* (The Youth's Magic Horn, 1805–8). In the final song of the *Wayfarer* cycle, the protagonist wanders out into the world, having taken leave of the girl who has rejected him. The dark heath and blossoming linden tree capture, respectively, his sentiments about the hopelessness of his present situation and his memories of a happier past.

Mahler plays on the musical conventions of Romantic song in ways that reflect a nascent Modernism. In an example of what has been called "progressive tonality," the song begins in E minor but ends in a remote F minor, traveling through C major and minor for the second stanza and F major for the third. The formal design of the song also reflects this open-ended quality. Unlike most Romantic poetry based on folk models, such as Heine's text for *Dichterliebe*

(Anthology 10), Mahler's text does not divide into units of equal length that suggest a strophic musical form, where the same melody is used for different stanzas. Yet the song at first seems to suggest a strophic form. The first three lines are set to a conventional eight-measure unit closing in the tonic. In measure 9, Mahler sets the words "O Augen blau" to the initial melodic-harmonic motive, as if starting another strophe. But two measures later the melody deviates, and it comes to a premature close after only six measures. After a transition and a turn to the key of C, the opening melodic phrase is heard again, but leads off in yet another direction. Now unfolding at a faster, more regular pace than the lugubrious opening, the vocal line and harmony shift uneasily between C major and minor. The final stanza of the poem, about the linden tree, is set to an entirely different melody in a new key, F major (m. 41), before concluding in F minor. (This theme that would reappear in the third movement of Mahler's First Symphony, where it is marked "very simple and plain, like a folk tune.")

Two other aspects of the song show Mahler's Modernist approach to Romantic conventions. First, his orchestration tends to be colorful but spare. He avoids a lush sound in order to highlight individual timbres or unusual combinations of instruments. Thus at the opening we hear only selected woodwinds—flutes, clarinets, English horn—and a harp. In the second stanza (m. 17) Mahler instructs all strings to play with mutes, then for a brief moment introduces a solo violin playing without mute (mm. 27–28).

Second, despite the strong feelings conveyed by the text, Mahler's music adopts a somewhat detached, even ironic tone—in the sense of seeming to go against the apparent meaning of the text. At the opening, and then twice later in the vocal part (mm. 25, 51), Mahler explicitly directs that the music be performed without any sentimentality. The steady dotted rhythms in the winds and the bass-and-chord accompaniment pattern (usually in the harp) give the song an inexorable, marchlike quality. Indeed, in his original manuscript Mahler wrote that the song was to be played "in the tempo of a funeral march." This idiom, as so often in Mahler, casts a somber veil over even the most lyrical elements of the song. The ultimate ironic twist comes after the singer has fallen silent on the word "dream." In the quiet (*ppp* and *pppp*) but heartbreaking final two measures of the song, the idyllic F-major memory of the past is pulled into the dark reality of F minor.

22

GIACOMO PUCCINI (1858–1924)

La bohème: Act 2, Musetta's Waltz

Opera, 1896

From Giacomo Puccini, *La Bohème, Vocal Score.* New York: Dover Publications, Inc.

13 MUSETTA — a Tempo

me,............. ricerca in me da ca _ po a piè;... (to his friends in a voice half choked by emotion)

MARCEL

Le _ ga _ temi al _ la

a Tempo

16
MUSETTA

sottolineando
ritenendo ....

ed as _ sa _ po _ ro al _ lor la bra _ mo _

ALCINDORO (on thorns)

Quel _ la gente che di _ rà?

MARCEL

seggiola!

ritenendo ....

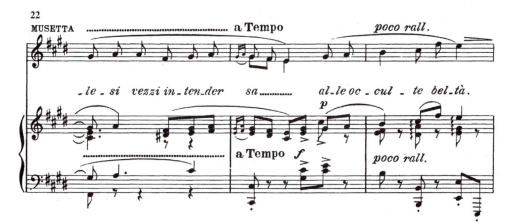

MUSETTA *flirtatious, turning intently toward Marcello, who is beginning to become agitated*

Quando me'n vo' soletta per la via,	When I go alone on the street,
la gente sosta e mira	people stop and stare
e la bellezza mia tutta ricerca in me	and everyone seeks my beauty in me
da capo a pie'....	from head to toe....
Ed assaporo allor la bramosia	And then I taste the subtle desire
sottil, che da gli occhi traspira	that shines from their eyes
e dai palesi vezzi intender sa	and from the outward charms can perceive
alle occulte beltà.	all the secret beauties.
Così l'effluvio del desìo tutta m'aggira,	Thus the flood of desire envelops me,
felice mi fa!	makes me happy!
E tu che sai, che memori e ti struggi	And you who know, who remember and try
da me tanto rifuggi?	to flee from me so?
So ben: le angoscie tue non le vuoi dir,	I know well: you don't want to share your sufferings,
ma ti senti morir!	but you feel like you're dying!

MARCELLO *to his friends*

Legatemi alla seggiola!	Tie me to the chair!

ALCINDORO

Quella gente che dirà?	What will these people say?
(Quel canto scurrile	(That scurrilous song
mi muove la bile!)	arouses my anger!)

MIMÌ *to Rodolfo*

Io vedo ben che quella poveretta	I see clearly that that poor girl
tutta invaghita ell'è,	is completely infatuated,
tutta invaghita di Marcel!	she's completely infatuated with Marcel!

Schaunard and Colline leave the table and stand on one side, watching the scene intently. Rodolfo and Mimì remain seated alone, talking. Marcello, ever more agitated, tries to go, but cannot resist Musetta's voice.

RODOLFO *to Mimì*

Marcello un dì l'amò.	One day Marcello loved her.

SCHAUNARD

Ah, Marcello cederà!	Ah, Marcello will give way!

COLLINE

Chi sa mai quel che avverrà!　　　　*Who knows what will happen!*

RODOLFO *to Mimì*

La fraschetta l'abbandonò　　　　　*That coquette left him*
per poi darsi a miglior vita.　　　　*to give herself to a better life.*

SCHAUNARD

Trovan dolce al pari il laccio　　　　*They find the snare equally sweet*
chi lo tende e chi ci dà.　　　　　　*the one who offers it and the one*
　　　　　　　　　　　　　　　　who is snared.

COLLINE

Santi numi, in simil briga　　　　　*Holy gods, in such trouble*
mai Colline intopperà!　　　　　　 *Colline will never fail!*

MUSETTA

(Ah! Marcello smania . . .　　　　　*(Ah! Marcello is agitated . . .*
Marcello è vinto!)　　　　　　　　*Marcello is beaten!)*

MIMÌ

(Quell'infelice mi muove a pietà!)　　*(That poor man moves me to pity!)*

ALCINDORO

Parla pian!　　　　　　　　　　　*Speak softly!*
Zitta, zitta!　　　　　　　　　　　*Quiet, quiet!*

COLLINE

(Essa è bella, io non son cieco,　　　*(She is beautiful, I am not blind,*
ma piaccionmi assai più　　　　　　*but I prefer*
una pipa e un testo greco!)　　　　　*my pipe and a Greek text!)*

MIMÌ *squeezing toward Rodolfo*

T'amo!　　　　　　　　　　　　　*I love you!*
Quell'infelice mi muove a pietà!　　　*That poor man moves me to pity!*
L'amor ingeneroso è tristo amor!　　 *Selfish love is sad love!*

RODOLFO *with his arms around Mimì's waist*

Mimì !	*Mimì!*
È fiacco amor quel che le offese	*Love is weak that cannot*
vendicar non sa!	*avenge offenses!*
Non risorge spento amor!	*Love that is gone does not rise again!*

ALCINDORO

Modi, garbo!	*Manners, tact!*
Zitta, zitta!	*Quiet, quiet!*

MUSETTA *to Alcindoro, in protest*

Io voglio fare il mio piacere!	*I want to do as I please!*
Voglio far quel che mi par,	*I want to do what I like,*
non seccar! non seccar!	*Don't bother me! Don't bother me!*

SCHAUNARD

(Quel bravaccio a momenti cederà!	*(That braggard will soon give way!*
Stupenda è la commedia!	*The comedy is stupendous!*
Marcello cederà!)	*Marcello will give way!)*

To Colline

Se tal vaga persona,	*If such a lovely girl*
ti trattasse a tu per tu,	*were to engage you intimately,*
la tua scienza brontolona	*your grumbling science*
manderesti a Belzebù!	*you'd send to the devil!*

MUSETTA

(Or convien liberarsi del vecchio!)	*(Now let's get free of the old man!)*

   pretending to feel a sharp pain

Ahi!	*Ouch!*

ALCINDORO

Che c'è?	*What is it?*

MUSETTA

Qual dolore, qual bruciore!	*What pain, what agony!*

ALCINDORO

Dove?	*Where?*

MUSETTA *showing her foot flirtatiously*

Al pie'!	*In my foot!*

He leans down to undo Musetta's shoe.

MARCELLO *greatly moved*

Gioventù mia,	*Oh my youth,*
tu non sei morta,	*you are not dead,*
né di te morto è il sovvenir!	*neither is the memory of you!*
Se tu battessi alla mia porta,	*If you were to knock at my door,*
t'andrebbe il mio core ad aprir!	*My heart would run to open it for you!*

MUSETTA

Sciogli, slaccia, rompi, straccia!	*Undo it, untie it, break it, tear it!*
Te ne imploro . . .	*I beg you . . .*
Laggiù c'è un calzolaio.	*There's a cobbler over there.*
Corri, presto!	*Run quickly!*
Ne vòglio un altro paio.	*I want another pair.*
Ahi! che fitta,	*Oh! what a pain,*
maledetta scarpa stretta!	*cursed tight shoe!*
Or la levo . . .	*Now I'll take it off . . .*

Takes off her shoe and puts in on the table.

Eccola qua.	*There it is.*
Corri, va, corri. Presto, va! va!	*Run, go run. Quickly, go! Go!*

ALCINDORO

Imprudente!	*Imprudent girl!*
Quella gente che dirà?	*What will people say?*

Trying to restrain Musetta

Ma il mio grado!	*But my position!*
Vuoi ch'io comprometta?	*You want me to be compromised?*

Quickly hides Musetta's shoes under his coat, which he then buttons up.

Aspetta ! Musetta! Vo'.	*Wait! Musetta! I'm going.*

Runs offstage quickly

SCHAUNARD AND COLLINE, THEN RODOLFO

La commedia è stupenda!	*The comedy is stupendous!*

Musetta and Marcello embrace passionately.

MUSETTA

Marcello!	*Marcello!*

MARCELLO

Sirena!	*Siren!*

SCHAUNARD

Siamo all'ultima scena!	*We're at the final scene!*

A waiter brings the bill.

RODOLFO, SCHAUNARD, AND COLLINE

Il conto?	*The bill?*

SCHAUNARD

Così presto?	*So soon?*

COLLINE

Chi l'ha richiesto?	*Who asked for it?*

SCHAUNARD *to the waiter*

Vediam!   *Let's see!*

After looking at the bill, he passes it to his friends.

—Giuseppe Giacosa and Luigi Illica

The segment from Act 2 of *La bohème* commonly known as Musetta's Waltz is one of the most innovative and effective scenes of nineteenth-century opera. The librettists Giacosa and Illica wrote their text in a natural conversational style, with short lines and frequent interjections. Puccini sets it as a fast-paced, collage-like superimposition of different musical ideas and actions. The result is very modern, showing the influence of a realist aesthetic that began to prevail in the latter part of the century. At the same time, the lyricism and formal coherence of the scene place it within the conventions of Italian opera that Puccini inherited from Verdi. Musetta's Waltz is solidly anchored in the key of E major and around the recurrence of a main theme.

Act 2 takes place on Christmas Eve in and around the Café Momus in the bustling Latin Quarter of Paris. The stage is packed with café patrons, waiters, students, shopkeepers, children, soldiers, and policemen. Within this frame, the main action focuses on the attempt of Musetta to win back her former lover, Marcello, and dump her current escort, the rich, elderly Alcindoro. To gain Marcello's attention in such a crowd, Musetta sings a seductive slow waltz. Like Carmen's *Habanera* (Anthology 16), it is diegetic music. That is, the waltz is heard as a song by the characters within the opera, including the other members of Musetta's circle of impoverished young artists—Mimì, Rodolfo, Schaunard, and Colline—who comment and react as it unfolds. Puccini thus creates a wonderfully complex musico-dramatic polyphony. Musetta's number (also like Carmen's) is a kind of siren song, and it works. As he listens, the smitten Marcello tells his friends to "tie me to the chair" (mm. 15–16) and later calls Musetta his "siren" (mm. 99–100), both clear references to the Odysseus legend.

After performing two strophes of the waltz (beginning with "Quando me'n vo," m. 1, and "E tu che sai," m. 33), Musetta executes the next part of her plan. With a *fortissimo* scream "Ahi!" (notated as nonpitched by Puccini, m. 78) she begins to complain so loudly about a (faked) pain in her foot that Alcindoro is embarrassed and soon goes rushing off to find a new pair of shoes, thus allowing Musetta and Marcello to reunite.

But even before they embrace, we know the outcome. In a brilliant stroke, Puccini has Marcello sing a third strophe of the waltz ("Gioventù mia," m. 82) while Musetta is raging about her shoe and other characters join in. The orchestra has the final word, playing the waltz one last time, triple *forte* and at a broader tempo (m. 96), as the waiter brings the bill and a marching band starts up offstage.

It is revealing to compare Puccini's approach to ensemble writing in *La bohème* with Verdi's in *Rigoletto* (Anthology 15). The basic technique is similar. Both composers present the emotions and actions of multiple characters simultaneously; both differentiate the characters with distinctive musical themes or lines. But while Verdi's is a private, intimate (and ultimately tragic) scene, based mainly on the juxtaposition of lyrical melodies, Puccini's is a large-scale, public spectacle in which lyrical melody (Musetta's waltz tune) is only one element among many. These include an amorous dialogue between Mimì and Rodolfo; private musings by the philosopher Colline about preferring his pipe and ancient Greek texts to beautiful women; mutterings of humiliation from Alcindoro; and yelps of mock pain from Musetta. It is this kind of superimposition that gives Puccini's scene its realistic atmosphere and carries it well beyond the traditions of earlier Italian opera.

ⓢ Norton Opera Sampler video available

23

CLAUDE DEBUSSY (1862–1918)

Fêtes galantes I: *En sourdine*

Song (*mélodie*), 1891

From Claude Debussy, *Fêtes Galantes*. Paris: J. Joubert.

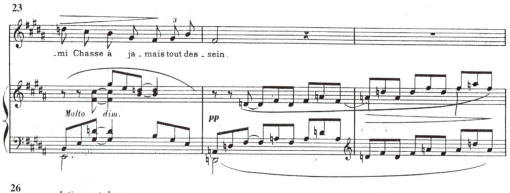

_mi Chasse à ja _ mais tout des _ sein.

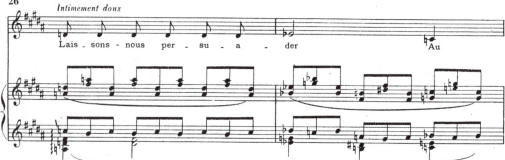

Lais _ sons - nous per _ su _ a _ der Au

souf _ fle ber _ ceur et doux Qui vient à tes pieds ri _

_ der Les on _ des de ga _ zon roux.

Et quand so _ len _ _ nel le soir, Des chê _ nes

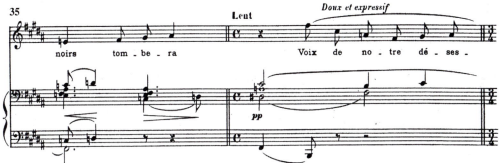

noirs tom _ be _ ra **Doux et expressif** Voix de no _ tre dé _ ses _

Lent

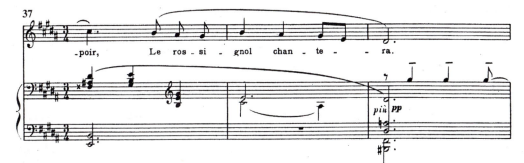

_poir, Le ros _ si _ gnol chan _ te _ ra.

En se perdant

Calmes dans le demi-jour	*Calm in the twilight*
Que les branches hautes font,	*Created by the high branches,*
Pénétrons bien notre amour	*Let our love be penetrated*
De ce silence profond.	*By this profound silence.*
Fondons nos âmes, nos coeurs	*Let us melt together our souls, our hearts,*
Et nos sens extasiés,	*And our ecstatic senses,*
Parmi les vagues langueurs	*Amidst the vague languors*
Des pins et des arbousiers.	*Of the pines and evergreens.*
Ferme tes yeux à demi,	*Close your eyes halfway,*
Croise tes bras sur ton sein,	*Cross your arms on your breast,*
Et de ton coeur endormi	*And from your slumbering heart*
Chasse à jamais tout dessein.	*Drive away forever any plan.*
Laissons-nous persuader	*Let us be persuaded*
Au souffle berceur et doux	*By the wind, rocking and gentle,*
Qui vient, à tes pieds, rider	*Which, at your feet, comes to rustle*
Les ondes des gazons roux.	*The waves of the russet grass.*
Et quand, solennel, le soir	*And when the evening solemnly*
Des chênes noirs tombera	*Falls from the dark oak trees,*
Voix de notre désespoir,	*Voice of our despair,*
Le rossignol chantera.	*The nightingale will sing.*

—Paul Verlaine

Like other French composers of his generation, Debussy was drawn to the poetry of Paul Verlaine (1844–1896), one of the most important figures associated with the Symbolist movement. Verlaine's verses strike a balance between delicacy and passion. They also display an inherent musicality. Verlaine treats the French language almost like a tonal system, fashioning his poems as much from the sonorous properties of words and syllables as from traditional meaning or syntax.

　　Debussy wrote two sets of songs (often called *mélodies* or *chansons*) on poems from Verlaine's collection *Fêtes galantes* (literally "gallant parties," referring to the leisurely pursuits of aristocrats in eighteenth-century France). Debussy responds to the unique qualities of the poems as only a great composer can. His Verlaine settings offer some of the subtlest fusions of word and tone in the history of Western music. Debussy's musical language is fundamentally tonal. *En sourdine* (Muted) ends in the notated key of B major, which is prepared by two measures of a dominant seventh harmony. Yet added tones tend to attenuate the chords and modify traditional diatonic progressions. As the vocal part ends, Debussy appends a ninth (G♯) to the dominant seventh (m. 39). That G♯ carries over to the final chord of the song, as a sixth "frozen" above the tonic triad.

The same G♯ also initiates *En sourdine*; in a gently syncopated rhythm it pushes off into the languid melody in the right hand of the piano. The first harmony of the song is neither tonic nor dominant, but a half-diminished seventh chord (E♯–G♯–B–D♯). This is the famous "Tristan" chord from the opening of Wagner's opera *Tristan und Isolde* of 1859. Debussy even takes over the exact pitches and spacing of Wagner's chord (though an octave higher than in the first measures of the *Tristan* Prelude). For most composers after Wagner, the "Tristan" chord became a sonic emblem of unfulfilled longing, of erotic passion unquenched. But Debussy saps the chord of much of its potential intensity and forward motion. In *En sourdine* it hovers, *pianissimo*, not so much "resolving" to the tonic B major as sinking on to it. We thus hear the difference between Debussy's early Modernist harmonic language and that of the Wagnerian style from which it develops.

The vocal style at the opening of *En sourdine* is also distinct from much nineteenth-century song. Instead of a conventional melody, Debussy creates a restrained, declamatory line that hovers on the note D♯ for almost two measures before moving on. Like his German contemporary Hugo Wolf (Anthology 11), although with a French sensibility, Debussy's practice reflects a naturalist aesthetic in which the vocalist sings speech rhythms rather than tunes shaped by purely musical principles. Of course, in Debussy's case the understated setting of the initial line also captures perfectly the meaning of Verlaine's words, "Calm in the twilight," as well as the sense of the poem's title, *Muted*.

Even though the poem divides into five four-line stanzas, each with the same design and rhyme scheme (*abab*), Debussy avoids any hint of a strophic musical structure (that is, the same setting for different stanzas). There is nonetheless in *En sourdine* a clear ternary shape based on contrast and return: **A** (mm. 1–17), **B** (mm. 18–31), **A'** (mm. 32–43). Debussy groups the first two stanzas together by tempo and mood (*Rêveusement lent*, slowly, as if in a dream), and by the recurrence of the piano motive of measures 1–4. Then, as the poet turns directly to the object of his, or her, affection with the command "Close your eyes" (m. 18), the tempo increases ("speeding up somewhat"), the texture is energized by flowing triplets in the piano, and the vocal line takes on greater lyrical intensity. This **B** segment comprises the third and fourth stanzas of the poem.

In the final stanza the poet steps back somewhat from the immediacy of the erotic encounter to reflect on what will happen next. Debussy treats this moment (m. 33) as a partial musical return by reintroducing the original piano motive (now accompanied on the first beat by a different half-diminished seventh chord) and a hint of the low, sustained D♯ in the voice. But for all that is new, the triplet rhythms of the more passionate **B** section have spilled over into **A'**. And there are other new elements, including a whole-tone complex in measure 35, with all six notes of the scale sounded between piano and voice (F♯–G♯–A♯–C♮–D♮–E♮). The calm spirit of the opening returns only in the piano postlude (mm. 39–41).

There is a powerful psychological realism in the way Debussy manages the return to **A'**. As humans we cannot simply shut out a moment such as that related by the poet in the third and fourth stanzas. Strong memories, like the insistent triplets, will continue to affect us.

READING AN ORCHESTRAL SCORE

CLEFS

The music for some instruments is written in clefs other than the familiar treble and bass. In the following example, middle C is shown in the four clefs used in orchestral scores:

The alto clef is primarily used in viola parts. The tenor clef is employed for cello, bassoon, and trombone parts when these instruments play in a high register.

TRANSPOSING INSTRUMENTS

The music for some instruments is customarily written at a pitch different from their actual sound. The following list, with examples, shows the transposing instruments that appear in this volume.

Instrument	Transposition	Written note	Actual sound
Piccolo	sounds an octave higher than written		
Trumpet in C	sounds as written		
Clarinet in B♭	sounds a major second lower than written		
Clarinet in A Trumpet in A Cornet in A	sound a minor third lower than written		
English horn Horn in F	sound a fifth lower than written		
Horn in E	sounds a minor sixth lower than written		
Horn in E♭	sounds a major sixth lower than written		
Contrabassoon Horn in C Double bass	sound an octave lower than written		
Bass clarinet in B♭ (written in treble clef)	sounds a major ninth lower than written		

INSTRUMENT NAMES AND ABBREVIATIONS

WOODWINDS

English	Italian	German
Piccolo (Picc.)	Flauto piccolo (Fl. picc.)	Kleine Flöte (Kl. Fl.)
Flute (Fl.)	Flauto (Fl.)	Flöte (Fl.)
Oboe (Ob.)	Oboe (Ob.)	Oboe (Ob.)
English horn (E. H.)	Corno inglese (Cor. ingl.)	Englisch Horn (Engl. Horn)
Clarinet (Cl.)	Clarinetto (Clar.)	Klarinette (Klar.)
Bass clarinet (B. cl.)	Clarinetto basso (Cl.b.)	Baßklarinette (Bkl.)
Bassoon (Bsn., Bssn.)	Fagotto (Fag.)	Fagott (Fag.)
Contrabassoon (C. bsn.)	Contrafagotto (Cfg.)	Kontrafagott (K-fg.)

BRASS

English	Italian	German
Horn (Hn.)	Corno (Cor.)	Horn (Hr., Hrn.)
Trumpet (Tpt.)	Tromba (Tr.)	Trompete (Trpt.)
Cornet (Cor.)	Cornetta (Ctta.)	Kornett
Alto trombone (A. trb.)	Alto trombone (A. trb.)	Alt Posaune (A-Pos.)

Trombone (Trb.),
    Tenor trombone (T. trb.)
	Trombone (Trb.),
	    Tenor trombone (T. trb.)
		Posaune (Pos.),
		    Tenor Posaune (T-Pos.)

Bass trombone (B. trb.)	Bass trombone (B. trb.)	Baß Posaune (B-Pos.)
Tuba (Tb.)	Tuba (Tb.)	Baßtuba (Btb.)

PERCUSSION

English	Italian	German
Kettledrums (K. D.)	Timpani (Timp.)	Pauken (Pk.)
Tam-tam (Tam)	Tam-tam (Tam)	Tamtam (Tamt.)

STRINGS

English	Italian	German
Violin (Vn., Vln.)	Violino (Viol.)	Violine (Viol.)
Viola (Va.)	Viola (Va.)	Bratsche (Br.), Viola (Vla.)
Violoncello, Cello (Vc.)	Violoncello (Vcllo.)	Violoncello, Cello (Vc., Vlc.)
Double bass (D. bs.)	Contrabasso (C. B.)	Kontrabaß (K. B., Kb.)

OTHER INSTRUMENTS

English	Italian	German
Harp (Hp.)	Arpa (Arp.)	Harfe (Hrf.)
Piano	Pianoforte (Pft.)	Klavier
Voice	Voce	Singstimme, Gesang

NOTE NAMES

English	Italian	German
C	do	C
C♯	do diesis	Cis
D♭	re bemolle	Des
D	re	D
D♯	re diesis	Dis
E♭	mi bemolle	Es
E	mi	E
E♯	mi diesis	Eis
F♭	fa bemolle	Fes
F	fa	F
F♯	fa diesis	Fis
G♭	sol bemolle	Ges
G	sol	G
G♯	sol diesis	Gis
A♭	la bemolle	As
A	la	A
B♭	si bemolle	B
B	si	H
B♯	si diesis	His
C♭	do bemolle	Ces

APPENDIX 3

GLOSSARY OF PERFORMANCE INDICATIONS

a   at, by
abbandono   with abandon
accelerando (accel.)   becoming faster
adagio   a slow tempo
affrettando   hurrying
agitato   agitated, excited
alla (all)   to the, in the style of
allargando (allarg.)   becoming slower and broader
allegretto   a moderately fast tempo
allegro   a rapid tempo
allmählig   gradual
an   on
ancora   once more
andante   a moderately slow tempo
andantino   a tempo slightly faster than *andante*
animant   becoming livelier
animato   animated
animé   becoming faster
appassionato   impassioned
appena   barely
arco   played with the bow
armonioso   harmoniously
assai   very
aus   out of

Ausdruck   expression
belebt   brisk
beschleunigend   becoming faster
bis   until
brillante   brilliant
col canto, colla voce   following the soloist
come sopra   as before
corta   short
crescendo (cresc.)   becoming louder
cupa   dark
Dämpfer   mute
decrescendo (decresc.)   becoming softer
délicatement   delicately
détaché   detached
devozione   devotion
di   of
diminuendo (dim., dimin.)   becoming softer
divisi (div.)   divided
dolce   sweetly
dolcissimo (dolciss.)   very sweetly
doux   sweetly
dumpf   hollow
e, ed   and
egualmente   equally

A7

eleganza elegance

en in

equivale equivalent

espansivo expansive

espressione with expression

espressivo (espr., espress.) expressive

et and

expressif expressive

feurig fiery

forza force

furioso raging

gedehnt stretched out

geheimnissvoll full of mystery

gestopft (gest.) stopped

getheilt (geth.) divided

getragen solemn

giusto fitting

grazia graceful

grell glaring

Griffbrett fingerboard

heftig heavy

immer always

incalzando pressing

innig tender

intimement intimately

lamentoso mournful

langsam slow

largamente broadly

larghetto the diminutive of *largo*, somewhat faster than *largo*

largo a very slow tempo

lebhaft lively

legatissimo very smooth

legato (leg.) smooth

leggierissimo very lightly

leggiero (legg.) lightly

leise soft

lento a slow tempo

maestoso majestic

marcato (marc.) with emphasis

marcia march

mässig moderate

m. d. right hand

mehr more, multiple

meno less

mezza half

m. g. left hand

mit with

moderato at a moderate tempo

moins less

molto very much

morendo dying away

mosso rapid

movimento movement

m. s. left hand

muta change

Nachschläge the two terminating notes at the end of a trill

nicht not

niente nothing

nimmt take

noch still

non not

offen open

ogni every

ohne without

ordine order

ouvert open

pedale (ped.) pedal

perdant losing

perdendosi dying away

pesante heavily

peu a little

piacere pleasure, discretion

più more

pizzicato (pizz.) plucked

plus more

poco little

portamento a continuous movement from one pitch to another

prima first

quarto fourth

quasi almost

rallentando (rall., rallent.) becoming slower

recitative (recit.) a singing style imitating speech

rêveusement dreamily

rinforzando (rfz, rin., rinforz.) with sudden emphasis

ritardando (rit., ritard) slowing

ritenuto (riten.) holding back

scherzando   playfully
schleppen   dragging
schlicht   plain
Schluss   cadence
schnell   fast
schwer   heavy
schwermüthigen   melancholic
secco (sec)   dry
seguono   accompanying
semplice   in a simple manner
sempre   always
senza   without
sforzando (sf, sfz)   with sudden emphasis
simile   in a similar manner
sino   until
smorzando (smorz.)   fading away
sordino   mute
sostenuto   sustained
sotto   under
sottolineando   emphasized
spiccato   bouncing the bow lightly off the string
staccato (stacc.)   detached
stentato (stent.)   loud
stingendo   fading
streng   strict
stretto   increasing speed
strillando   screaming
stringendo   becoming faster

sul   on
sustenuto   sustained
Takt   beat
tanto   many
tenero   tender
tenuto (ten.)   sustained
toujours   always
tranquillo   tranquil
trattenuto (tratt.)   slowed down
tremolo (trem.)   rapid reiteration of one or more notes
trois   three
tutti   all
ultimo   last
un   a
und   and
unisono (unis.)   unison
verklingend   fading away
verlöschend   dying out
vivace, vivo   lively
vite   fast
voce   voice
wechselvoll   oscillating
weich   soft
wieder   again
zu   to
zurückhaltend   holding back